WARRIORS RIS3

Terri S. Van Slyke

Do not gloat over me, my enemy!
Though I have fallen, I will rise.
Though I sit in darkness,
the Lord will be my light.

MICAH 7:8

Janine Chellington Press
Literature with Depth and Elegance

Special thanks to Mom, Dad, Janine Chellington Press, Jennifer Toelle, Barb Dennis, and to the community of Albany, Missouri.

Janine Chellington Press, L.L.C. | Central Kansas.

ISBN: 979-8-9906048-6-5

For Mom and Dad, thank you for your unwavering love and support. Most importantly, thank you for showing me and teaching me the unconditional love, grace, and mercy of Jesus.

TABLE OF CONTENTS

1

THE DEFEAT

XIX

It was a Good Friday.
A day much like today.
When my heart stopped beating,
And the bounce began to fade.

The darkness that engulfed me,
Was but a gloomy loss of thee,
My chest indefinitely tightened.
How could this even be?

Rain poured within my soul.
To a point, I'll drown no more.
For tomorrow, I can no longer see.
A world with dreams and goals.

Clutched my hand through thick and thin,
Hardwood heaven full of sin.
For you, I bled, cried, and prayed.
But you claimed my spirit yet again.

God forgive me and forgive those,
Who entertain demons from a self-righteous throne.
Ruling with a wicked tapestry of fake integrity.
"Why am I forsaken?!" I sobbed alone.

For the love of the game I gave my life.
Was this all for naught but only strife.
I never fathomed I'd turn my head,
And lodged in my back, alas...
                    A KNIFE.

Kelly set her pen aside. It had been years since she felt the satisfaction of writing something of value. Kelly found peace in writing and basketball; they helped her deal with the frustrations of life. Even as a kid, writing and shooting hoops helped alleviate her stress and tension.

Recently, Kelly's life had been in shambles. She was completely overwhelmed with anxiety, depression, and uncertainty. This time of year, she'd normally be immersed in a coach's organized chaos of playbooks, workout programs and recruits' statistics. The absence of this organized chaos left her filling a void by writing out her emotions. As she mulled over her words once again, she wondered what she should title this elegy of emotions. Kelly sighed, picked up her pen, and simply wrote the title as XIX.

The number nineteen held immense significance for Kelly. This number stood for failure and defeat and perfectly described the overwhelming emotions she felt this past year. These emotions flooded her brain, transporting her back to her most challenging day when she felt basketball had ended in her life.

"Why? I still don't understand any of this," she whispered aloud to herself. Tears welled in her eyes as she flashed back to Good Friday, April 19th, of the previous year.

With Easter weekend coming up, Kelly—a woman of strong faith—couldn't wait, as it was one of her favorite holidays. She cherished the weekend celebrations and the fellowship with family and friends at church on Easter Sunday. On this particular Good Friday, Kelly felt a sense of renewal. It was a beautiful Friday morning. The sun was shining. The birds were chirping. The essence of the newly blossomed flowers filled the air. As the sun beamed on the dew of the freshly cut green grass, Kelly thought the entire scene was a veritable feast for the eyes. What

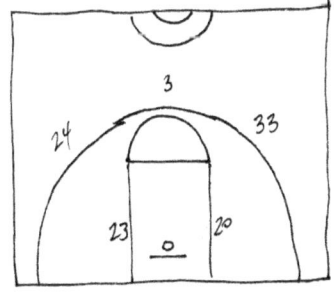

a beautiful day to be on campus, closing a year of hard work. A new chapter began today as a promising group of recruits would arrive with the opportunity to make their commitment to the Lions Park University basketball program next season. Today was the day where she knew the pendulum was finally swinging in her favor.

Getting out of her car, Kelly noticed how pristine the campus looked. She thought to herself that her life was aligning in such a beautiful environment. The campus sat atop a hill nestled in the suburbs, bordered by a sprawling city park. For campus events, the grounds were meticulously manicured—freshly mowed and mulched, with vivid spring blooms filling large planters and the spaces between buildings. At the base of the hill, the student center and athletic facilities stood—a modest structure, yet open and airy. Inside, school pride radiated from every wall, with vibrant colors, logos, and images of past athletes proudly on display. The gym carried a faint scent of fresh varnish, and the basketball court shimmered under the lights—in fact, it glistened.

Yes, magic was certainly going to happen today!

A beautiful day, an immaculate university she now called **home** and a great group of recruits.

A few years prior, Kelly took over a basketball team who was in complete disarray. Facing a tough situation, she stepped in to restore a program within a short time frame of a few months. It was by no means an easy task for anyone, especially for a coach who was early in her new career. With only one returning player, Kelly scrambled to find warm bodies to fill the roster. It was a challenging year, as many of her players had very little experience. Kelly knew this would be a process in which she would have to be patient and have faith in a brighter future.

Over the past two seasons, the team made steady progress. Though it lagged to meet Kelly's vision. The task was far from over: her team was short on recruits and training. As a coach, she focused on intelligent athletes with self-discipline and potential leadership. She wanted her team to make an impact both on and off the court. On this particular day, she was scheduled to sign athletes she believed were the key missing pieces to her program. There was a promising feeling the team she was assembling would build a healthy trust and rapport. Basketball was her life and her purpose. It was her heaven on Earth, and today the mission seemed to be finally falling into place.

She finished prepping for the recruits' arrival and walked down the hall of the athletics suite to prepare to welcome them upon their arrival. There was a lounge in the athletics suite that she decided would be the ideal place to relax for a few moments before the visit was underway. This was a space the team would often utilize when watching game film or gathering to watch March Madness. It was a comforting place, and Kelly needed to calm her nerves and excitement. As she sat down and turned on the television, she heard someone calling her name.

"Ms. Janssen," a voice echoed from an office nearby.

"Yes?" Kelly responded as she turned around to look down the hall at who was calling her.

"Would you please come in here for a minute?" the voice inquired. She recognized it was the voice of the athletic director, so she got up and walked into his office.

"Oh, hey, boss!" Kelly joked. "You scared me a little with your serious tone."

During their short time working together, the athletic director and Kelly built a supportive and encouraging rapport. Kelly frequently volunteered to assist with athletic events, whether by helping run games or preparing for major competitions. The athletic director also valued her expertise in the college admissions, recruitment, and compliance processes and often sought her input when working with other coaches and athletic recruits. Their conversations regularly touched on sports, local and prospective players, and more personal topics, including their shared faith.

The athletic director seemingly ignored her playful quip and continued to look at his computer and asked, "would you have a minute this afternoon to meet?"

Kelly quickly responded, "I'm signing recruits early in the afternoon, but I think we should be done around four o'clock? What is this about?"

The athletic director dismissed her question. Instead, he responded with a serious and stern look upon his face, "Yes, four will work. We can meet here." He then broke eye contact and immediately turned his eyes back to his computer.

Kelly, dumbfounded, said, "Okay." She turned to exit his office. She was taken aback, turned back to look at him and said, "I mean... yes, yes, that sounds good. I will see you then."

The athletic director briefly looked up at her, nodded, and went back to working at his computer.

Immediately, Kelly felt a sinking feeling in her stomach. Something felt off. First, the athletic director normally called her "Coach Janssen" or just "Coach." She questioned why he called her "Ms. Janssen." This seemed bizarre. She began obsessing over recent conversations earlier in the week. She figured she was over analyzing everything, but this interaction now made her head spin. Something seemed amiss. Suddenly, her bright outlook appeared cloudy.

Before her meeting, the afternoon was a total blur. Kelly struggled to focus on her recruits. Her mind wandered to what the athletic director wanted to talk about. He seemed upset and annoyed with her all week. He unexpectedly snapped at her during a baseball game the weekend prior when she was keeping score. At an athletic donor event two nights before Good Friday, he introduced other coaches to the donors and bragged on their accomplishments, but he failed to introduce her to anyone. He barely said two words to her the entire evening. She felt insignificant, but attributed his behavior to the demands of the month of April. She recalled when she brought her recruits by his office during their afternoon campus tour to say hello; he was very short with her. He normally spent time with the recruits, praising the basketball program and her coaching. This time he spent less time; he gave them his card and encouraged them to contact him if they had questions. Kelly felt this was weird and she felt invisible in the equation. She took a deep breath in to clear her mind. She finished her meetings with the recruits, attempting to maintain focus on the basketball program and the promising athletes.

Several of the recruits committed during the day. It was an achievement to have signed twice as many players for the upcoming season, because the previous year had been rough. Despite this progress, Kelly had an unsettling feeling something was wrong. As she made her trek down the hallway to the Athletic Director's office a few minutes before her meeting, one of her returning players passed by her in the hallway.

"Hey coach!" the player said, walking to her on-campus job in the Athletics Office. "Did a lot of the recruits commit?"

"Hi, Grace," Kelly said in a solemn tone. "And yes."

This was not the reaction Grace had anticipated by Coach Janssen. There was something about her that seemed not quite right. Grace paused. "Are you okay?"

Kelly smirked, trying to hide her racing anxiety. "I'm fine, Grace. I've got a meeting," she replied. Kelly had a horrible poker face. Her facial expressions often gave away her mood and her thoughts. Of all her players, the coach's emotions were always an open book to Grace.

Kelly continued walking down the hallway. Her steps aligned with her heartbeat. She opened the door to the athletic director's office, and at 4:19 p.m. on April 19.

COACH KELLY JANSSEN'S BASKETBALL WORLD WAS WRECKED TO THE CORE.

Kelly fled the athletic director's office, trying to contain composure until she was out of sight. She uncharacteristically walked right past Grace without even acknowledging her presence. Grace felt like something was very wrong. She turned to look down the hallway as the athletic director left his office and was walking towards her.

"Hi Grace," he said in a sober tone.

Grace definitely knew at this point something happened. The athletic director never called her by her first name. He always yelled in an excited and yet annoying way, "Hey, Villanueva!" This time, he seemed very distant.

"Rough day, sir?" Grace asked.

"Just business," the athletic director replied.

Grace's heart sank. She knew what "just business" meant. Between the athletic director's comments and Coach Janssen's eyes and body language, she feared she had just lost her beloved coach.

Kelly choked back tears as she fled the building. Ironically, the weather had drastically shifted while she was in her meeting. It was now pouring rain. She welcomed the downpour—it was a blessing. The rain shower disguised her swiftly streaming tears as the floodgates of her emotional control gave out. By the time she climbed into her car, she was soaked.

As Kelly slammed her car door shut, she hysterically screamed, "ARE YOU SERIOUS?! Of all the days to do this, he chose Good Friday?!" Kelly leaned forward until her forehead hit the steering wheel. Tears and raindrops blended as they dripped down her cheeks running to the floorboard.

She felt lost.
She felt nauseous.

She did not know where she should go or what she should do. Her head was spinning, ruminating on what had just transpired. Swirling memories from the breadth of her coaching height to this moment tormented her mind. She remembered the first time she parked in the athletics parking lot - the first day she went to an open gym. This parking lot, once a symbol of new beginnings, now marked the end. Unable to endure the pain any longer, she leaned back into the driver's seat, started her car, and sped away.

2

IMMERSION

Growing up, Kelly's parents owned property at the Lake of the Ozarks, and she cherished spending time there. However, a scary childhood experience — falling in the lake at age five — gave her a deep-seated fear of drowning. This fear showed up frequently in the form of recurring nightmares. In her nightmares, she found herself struggling to stay afloat in the middle of the lake, gasping for air as water filled her lungs. Some nights, she dreamt of a guiding light piercing through the darkness of the water, offering hope. Just as she began to sink, a saving hand would reach out, pulling her to safety, reassuring her everything would be alright.

In her most haunting dream, she found herself submerged in absolute darkness, enveloped by silence and stillness beneath the water's surface. It was a strange mixture of serenity and terror, leaving her feeling numb, hopeless, and oddly at peace all at once. As she glimpsed above the water, she saw a faint light. The realization her lungs were desperate for air set in, and she began to struggle. Just as she reached her breaking point, a figure materialized above the water's edge, gazing down at her struggling. Stretching her arm towards the surface, she pleaded for salvation, convinced this person would rescue her. But, to her dismay, the figure turned away, leaving her to her fate. With her final breath slipping away, she would jolt awake, gasping for air, clinging to the safety of her bed.

Losing her coaching job was a living nightmare, and it was mirrored in her awful dreams, making it tough to cope. Life was unbearable sometimes. She felt totally betrayed by people she thought she could trust. Her sense of purpose was shattered. She likened herself to a bobber in the lake, except she felt like the bobber in this game of life.

Writing became a therapeutic source of comfort for Kelly. Through the written word,

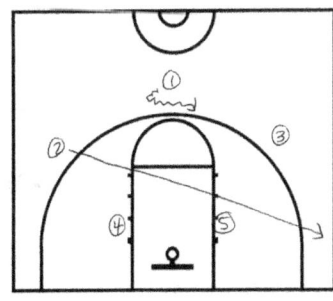

she was hungry to uncover what had gone awry. The comfort found by writing did not warrant a full escape as she would have liked. Since she still held another position on campus as an admissions recruiter, she was constantly reminded of the fact she was no longer coaching. There was no way to separate the pain; Every day for months, walking by the gymnasium during campus tours or other daily tasks was like a knife immediately puncturing her heart, twisting and twisting, just to make her bleed and die all over again inside. Even though it might've been in her head, she still felt like people were whispering about how she'd failed. Being on campus was, well, awkward.

Kelly occupied herself in her elaborate pen loops—every word made her think more deeply about herself. As she journeyed further into self-reflection, she became convinced coaching college basketball was her true calling. The absence of her coaching position tore her apart. Organizing basketball plans and breaking down game film should have been her immersion. Instead, she was seeking solace in writing. Through her prose it was as if fate itself were guiding her towards basketball.

Alone at home, she continuously replayed the year leading up to April 19 over and over in her mind. As she did so, over and over again, she found herself furious at God— she questioned how He could take away the only thing she ever truly loved. She would stand in the shower for what seemed like hours just sobbing and screaming at God.

"WHERE ARE YOU, GOD?!" SHE WOULD OFTEN SCREAM.

"YOU PROMISED ME YOU WOULD NEVER LEAVE ME.

WHERE ARE YOU?!!"

Kelly had fleeting moments of confidence, but then in a split second, it would dissipate. An overwhelming sense of discouragement and anxiety often led to panic attacks. It was confusing, frustrating, and discouraging; she didn't understand why she'd always revisit those terrible memories. Her confidence was shaken and her self-worth disintegrated. She slipped further into depression.

She felt like a fraud. She consistently told her players to not allow their self-worth to be attached to a person, an object, or a mistake. She wasn't practicing what she preached. Now, she questioned the philosophies she taught. She sighed and said aloud, "no wonder you took this away from me, God."

Feeling worse and in dire need of a distraction, Kelly started rummaging in her home office through her desk drawers to take her mind off of her current circumstances. As she reached to the back of the top drawer, she felt something lodged between the top and middle drawer. She slowly pulled the item out—it was an old Polaroid. The 30-year-old photo was a bit blurry, yet the memory was anything but faded in Kelly's mind. The photo featured Kelly standing in a driveway with her childhood best friend. That day, everything changed for her.

30-year-old Polaroid — Kelly & Jill, 1989
Kelly, age 6.

Looking at the photograph, stirs Kelly's mind flooding back suppressed with memories and emotions.

Kelly, her friend Jill, and Jill's older brother were dribbling a basketball around in the driveway. As the children played, they saw Kelly's mom, Anne, walking up the sidewalk towards them. There was a heaviness in Anne's steps as she approached Kelly. Her usually cheerful mom seemed really down.

"Kelly," her mom said somberly. "It's time to go."

This was the day the Janssens moved to a new town. She was terrified to leave the only life she had known in Kansas and move to a new state. She didn't want to move, but her dad was offered an opportunity to finally open his own business back in his hometown. Kelly's family drove off to begin a new life in Missouri.

Kelly stared at the photograph—the Polaroid she was now tightly grasping as she mentally transported back to the present day. "Woah," she said out loud to herself. She decided to turn it over and look at the back of the photo. The date was written, "04-19-1989." What a sinister coincidence, she thought. This memory was particularly difficult, because it brought back a heartbreaking experience.

Kelly found it difficult to adjust to this new place she was now to call "home." Elementary school in this town was much different from the private school she once attended which was a safe haven of acceptance and growth. She felt like an outsider and was continuously reminded of this fact by the cliques and different groups kids gravitate towards. Being quiet and shy made it hard for her to make friends. She felt alone.

After a few years, her dad's new business failed, and her family began to struggle financially. Kelly's parents tried their best to shield her from the hardships they were facing, but she could sense the difficulties. In a world obsessed with societal stereotypes and material possessions, gossip about her family's financial status spread rapidly through the community and into her school. She was bullied for being "the poor kid," and her parents experienced shunning from the community.

The Janssens faced hardship as they grappled with managing their finances. Life was often bleak, yet Kelly's parents clung to their faith, believing by God's grace, things would improve. There was a looming fear of not having enough food or losing their home. They showed this faith by giving their last $20 to those in even greater need. Her parents explained by relying on God and trusting in His provision was essential. This act of giving left a lasting impression on Kelly, because it was a testimony of having faith.

When Kelly was 9-years-old, her family was on the move yet again. Her dad, Axel, found a new job in Albany, Missouri. Axel traveled ahead of Kelly and Anne to get things settled in their new home. Kelly prayed this move would be better than the last. They all were hopeful about a new beginning. When Kelly and her mother, Anne, arrived at their new home, Kelly noticed immediately there was a basketball goal in the driveway.

"Mom!" Kelly exclaimed. "There's a basketball goal!"

"There sure is, Kelly," Anne replied. "I think this is God's way of telling you that everything is going to be okay."

The next day, her parents went to the local department store and bought her a basketball. She spent hours shooting in the driveway. Her dad would play H-O-R-S-E with her when he got off of work. He was a bit surprised how good she was at nine-years-old, especially when she began to regularly beat him.

Life finally seemed like it was swinging in a more optimistic direction for the Janssens. Home life, on the other hand, was becoming more and more complicated. Kelly's mom struggled with physical health issues and depression for the majority of Kelly's young life, but this seemed different. Anne was now fighting a new mental health battle. Just when they thought they were overcoming one storm in their life, they now faced something new and terrifying. Neither Kelly nor Axel really knew how to cope and help Anne heal.

The stigma of mental illness created fear in Kelly's parents. They did not want to disclose what was going on in their family. People often have the wrong perception of mental illness, which leads to misunderstandings about what those with mental illness really go through. This ever-present stigma, once someone receives a mental illness label, makes things even more difficult, especially in small communities. They feared if anyone discovered the truth of Anne's diagnosis Kelly would be removed from their home. Kelly was terrified to tell anyone about what she had dealt with daily.

When Kelly was in the fifth grade, her mom drove her to a new friend's house in the country for a birthday party. As Anne was having difficulty finding the house to drop Kelly off, she began to have a panic attack. Kelly knew how this incident would set her mom into a downward spiral. This was not the first breakdown Kelly witnessed with her mom, and it certainly would not be the last. Although Kelly was young, she was wise beyond her years, and her instinct was to reassure her mom.

She looked into Anne's eyes and said, "Mom, it's okay. It's not a big deal. I'm fine. We are here. Don't do anything stupid."

When Kelly arrived home later in the evening, her mom apologized. "Sweetie, I'm so sorry I got so upset and ruined your birthday party," Anne said. "But thank you for saying what you did. You kept mommy from doing something bad."

"Mama, you didn't ruin anything," Kelly fired back. "You yell at me when I say negative things about myself, so why do you put yourself down?"

This was a common interaction between Kelly and her mom throughout Kelly's upbringing. Kelly firmly believed she was the reason her mom restrained from doing something irrational and causing harm to herself. From this point forward, she developed a belief she could save her mom. Kelly developed a superhero-like complex, dedicated to saving her mom and anyone else struggling like her.

Throughout her teenage years, Kelly carried a heavy burden. She was often seen as wise beyond her years, a maturity shaped not by choice but by the realities of a life which demanded she grow up far sooner than most her age. Not only did she feel others could not relate to her daily experiences–there was no one for her to confide in during her mom's episodes. There was a looming fear this information would expose what her family chose to keep a private matter. Conversations about her mom's illness with her dad were rare, as Kelly recognized the weight it placed on him. And so, basketball became her refuge.

As Kelly matured into an adult and pursued her career, it was no surprise she chose a helping profession. However, her superhero complex now bore a new weight. Working with college students brought challenges she never envisioned. As an admissions recruiter, Kelly was often the first friendly face these students encountered, and she had a gift for connecting with people. She became their go-to person on campus because they knew she would guide them. Having already helped them make one of the most significant decisions of their lives, they trusted her. The burdens these students carried were heavy: depression, suicidal thoughts, self-harm, death, pregnancies, rape, drug and alcohol abuse, physical and verbal abuse, and heartbreaks were just some of the issues students faced. She inadvertently counseled them during the height of their struggles.

As she was a dedicated listening ear, Kelly absorbed a piece of each student's burden. She was naïve in thinking she could take on the responsibility of carrying their burdens for them. Each piece piled on top of her own burdens. This load was immensely heavy—weighing so much she would eventually begin to crack.

LOSING HER COACHING JOB WAS THE EXTRA WEIGHT THAT FINALLY BROKE HER.

Kelly now sat sobbing on her bedroom floor, **clutching the photograph** took her mentally to places she had long avoided. Her thoughts were scattered, and God was silent. Panic set in as she struggled to see a way out of her despair. Hopelessness infiltrated her mind, triggering a panic attack. She had fleeting moments of fear she would develop the same mental health issues her mom experienced.

As she gasped for air, Kelly felt an overwhelming sense of isolation, the weight of years of the multitude of unspoken worries pressing down on her. In a moment of darkness, she felt like she died when she was drowning in her dreams.

A spark of light flickered within her. She came to the realization she could not continue this way. She needed to find a way to heal and reclaim her life. She wiped her tears, her hands trembling, knowing asking God for help was her first step to healing. As she rose from the floor, a resolve formed within her—she was determined to find her way back to the surface and the shining light from above.

3

HARDWOOD HEAVEN

A shining light in Kelly's life was her blessing of natural athletic ability, and she loved sports. Kelly's love of basketball began when her Grandma Elaine gave her a Larry Bird Lil' Sport Basketball Hoop on her second birthday. This present was truly love at first sight. Kelly loved watching college and professional basketball with Grandma Elaine. They shared an adoration for Larry Bird and Michael Jordan. It was a connection she valued throughout her childhood until Grandma Elaine died of cancer when Kelly was a preteen. Basketball was an avenue for Kelly to keep her grandma close.

BASKETBALL MADE KELLY FEEL ALIVE.

Albany was a godsend for Kelly; she felt a profound sense of belonging. She found an avenue in sports that was a life-changing situation for her. She spent hours in the driveway shooting baskets. Like most youth, she pretended she would hit the game-winning shot with seconds left on the clock to win a championship. By high school, she was a multi-sport athlete, landing a spot on the varsity basketball team as a freshman. She worked hard over the summer to improve her game, taking notes from her coaches, and applying skills she had learned watching and practicing basketball. She was more than willing to do the dirty work on the court. Practicing those non-trackable stats—diving for loose balls, setting solid screens, securing strong box outs, giving max effort on every play and drill, and locking down players on defense. Soon, she made a name for herself on the court as a defensive specialist.

By her sophomore year, Kelly was a starting guard/small forward for the state-ranked Albany Warriors, and she held onto this role throughout the rest of her high school career. The Warriors were a well-disciplined team and had

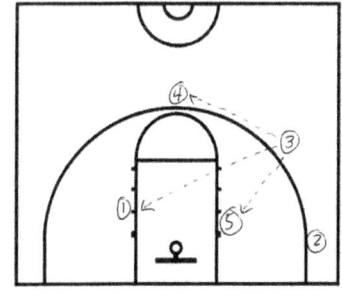

tremendous chemistry. They set school records. Kelly may not have lit up the scoring column, but it became clear she was the glue holding the team together. She did the little things on the court all in an effort for the team's success. By her senior year, the Warriors became the first team from her school to make the state's Final Four and championship weekend.

Kelly's devotion to being a top-notch defender attracted the attention of several college coaches. She ultimately accepted a scholarship to an NAIA college to chase her dream of playing college basketball. After college, she pursued a journalism career focusing on sports. Covering games and interviewing coaches and players only increased her longing to get involved with basketball in a different capacity. She could never quite explain it, but she felt a spiritual connection with the game. It was only by an accidental run-in with a college administrator who turned her career in a direction to become a college recruiter and to coach college basketball.

The past year had been a monotonous daily reminder of what she once had. As much as she tried to escape the feeling of not being consumed with basketball, she just could not shake it. She had applied to several college coaching jobs in the area, but nothing panned out. By October, the season was starting, and Kelly gave up on finding something this year. Instead, she worked on improving as a coach by attending coaching webinars, reading leadership and coaching books, and getting more involved with organizations which specialized in professional development in coaches. Although her confidence was shaken, she knew she needed to focus on her personal growth to be the best version of herself.

"Maybe I just need to take a break from basketball," she said aloud to herself after receiving a rejection email.

This was not the first time she felt like basketball had stabbed her in the back. College basketball was a challenging experience to say the least. Her high school team was incredibly successful, but her college team was the complete opposite. It was a foreign experience for Kelly.

During preseason her freshman year of college, she suffered an injury to her knee, one which required surgery. During surgery, it was discovered the cartilage damage was so severe there was nothing to be done to fix it. She spent a majority of her freshman season doing rehabilitation in the fitness center and training room, which also made it hard to connect with her teammates. Between the lack of success, suffering a devastating ACL (Anterior Cruciate Ligament) injury the following year, and a coaching change after her freshman year, the idea of continuing to play was no longer a good fit—especially mentally. She made the difficult decision heading into her junior season to end her playing career early.

This experience now felt all too familiar. Another moment of feeling like basketball turned its back on her after all of the blood, sweat, and tears she had given it. Months had passed since she last picked up a basketball. It was too heartbreaking, which made her really question herself of why she was having such a hard time moving on. "It's just a game," she constantly said to herself.

"This is a part of the profession. Coaches get fired all the time," her dad reminded her when she called to check in with her parents. "This isn't the end. This is nothing compared to the countless experiences you've been through in your life. Suck it up, Kel." She knew her dad was right.

On the one-year anniversary of losing her coaching job, she needed basketball more than ever. It was a roller coaster of a day. She felt extreme sadness and uncertainty about who she was and what her purpose on this Earth was to be. She thought perhaps it was time for her to run to the only place where she felt like she could forget about everything—an outdoor basketball court. Much like the Good Friday a year ago, it was a sunny day. The air was still. The temperature was in the mid-60s. It was a perfect day to find an outdoor court and let off some steam. After remembering so many hard memories, she felt like she needed to sweat.

But she didn't crave just any sweat—she desired the cold sweat she remembered from childhood, the kind when a fever finally broke and her system flushed the infection, bringing with it a rush of relief and renewed energy. Now, she needed a similar kind of release. She wanted the stress and tension of the past year drained from her body and mind so she could finally move on.

After a self-pep talk, Kelly made her way to a community park near her home. She had never been there, even though her house was nearby. It was desolate, but it had a basketball court. On the edge of the park, there sat a blacktop slab with two double rimmed basketball goals. The asphalt was worn and infiltrated with small cracks and weeds, yet it was smooth enough to dribble with ease. Paint once distinctly defined the common lines on a basketball court. However, those lines had long faded to a point of only providing a faint glimpse of what was.

The aesthetics of this court gave her flashbacks to her hometown court; she had practically grown up improving her game on the court. There was something majestic and beautiful about a blacktop like this one. It transported Kelly to where she fell in love with the game. It took her back to the moment of being a little girl and the joy she experienced playing. The court sat in a valley of a hill that led up to a house, just like the blacktop Kelly would run down her backyard slope to spend her afternoons shooting away stress. It was comforting and curiously familiar.

The court was not extraordinary, yet Kelly found solitude there. She spent hours enjoying the fresh air, shooting and escaping from the stresses of the daily grind. Kelly found it strange every time she came to play, no one was there. Either the local hoopers thought it was too rundown or it was a hidden treasure she was blessed to find.

This day, the blacktop was again vacant, so Kelly started her typical pre-workout activities—form shooting and dynamic stretching. She quickly learned at her age, it was beneficial for her body's recovery to get moving before trying to rattle off a bunch of layups and jumpers. She's not as agile as her teenage years. If she didn't stretch, she would be reminded of it the next day or two by her muscle soreness.

Kelly completed her pre-workout and began her form shooting, followed by some casual 10-15-feet jumpers. She started to feel the sensation of the love of basketball again. After about 30 minutes on the court, Kelly's cell phone rang. She usually would not answer a call during a workout, but something inside her nudged her to pick up.

"Hello?" she answered.

"KJ! It's Peyton! How are you?!" exclaimed the caller.

"Hey, Peyton, what's going on?!" Kelly replied in an ecstatic tone.

It was evident when Kelly reconnected with people from her past based on the nicknames they had for her. Former teammates she grew up with always called her KJ. It was a nickname she picked up early on in her organized basketball career—a nickname given to her by long-time teammate and friend, Peyton Murphy.

Peyton was a feisty, out-spoken, charismatic point guard. She was exceedingly confident, but not cocky. Peyton was the all-star, all-everything scorer and vocal leader. Off the court, she was just as talented in the classroom. She was athletic, artistic, smart, beautiful, and the all-around girl next door. Everyone in the state of Missouri knew of Peyton Murphy. Peyton was humble and graceful in dealing with all the press and attention. She received multiple offers to play Division 1 college basketball, but unfortunately, an injury crippled her career beyond high school.

Kelly was the lead-by-example, blue collar defender. Her tenacity and work ethic made Kelly who she was as a player. She may have been quiet vocally, but her game spoke volumes to true basketball enthusiasts. Kelly and Peyton had similar attributes, except Kelly lacked self-confidence. On the court their personalities were polar opposite, but their team chemistry was unrivaled.

Although they were in the same class, Peyton was almost a year older than Kelly. They grew up down the street from each other and became best friends. Peyton started driving a year earlier than Kelly, and she'd usually give her a ride to school and practices.

Kelly recalls their typical high school conversations:

"Honestly, KJ, I don't know what you would do without me. You would never make it to practice," Peyton joked.

"Well, if I wasn't there, who would save your butt all those times you get beat on defense," Kelly retorted.

"That's fair. Okay, I guess I'll continue to give you rides," Peyton quipped back with a smirk.

Kelly and Peyton understood one other and never passed judgment. They also held each other accountable, both on the court and in the classroom. There was an unspoken connection between them. By constantly challenging and encouraging one another, they were a successful duo both at friendship and on the court.

They lost touch in college and their 20s, but reconnected a couple of years before Kelly lost her coaching job. College basketball did not go as planned for either player. They both struggled in different ways without the other. Peyton watched her career diminish as recurring knee injuries, including a couple of instances of tearing her ACL in both knees, forced her to retire prematurely. Kelly found her shot and was becoming an all-star in her own right, only to watch it fade as a coaching change in her sophomore year created an atmosphere of abusive turmoil on the court. As the toxic environment raged on, Kelly also experienced an ACL injury as she was just getting back to her old self on the court after her knee injury the year before. Tearing her ACL, in addition to the toxic culture, solidified her decision to walk away from basketball.

Peyton moved back to their hometown a few years after completing her Master's degree. She landed a job as the Community Economic Developer and coached basketball as an assistant for their high school team. She married her grad school sweetheart and was raising three young boys with her husband.

Kelly, on the other hand, was married to the game of basketball. Her life was so consumed with her love of the game; other relationships were pushed to the back burner. She attempted dating, but she could never quite let her heart allow anyone to be a part of her life because basketball consumed her. Mostly, Kelly felt happy. She was doing something she loved.

Rekindling a friendship with Peyton was an absolute blessing to Kelly. Her positivity aided in Kelly staying above water mentally. Kelly admired Peyton, and Kelly was Peyton's security blanket. Peyton's game was at its best when Kelly was on the court. Peyton just knew Kelly always had her back, and Kelly knew Peyton had hers.

"I was thinking about you today, and I realized I need to call you for our monthly wellness check," said Peyton as their conversation continued. Besides her gifts on the basketball court, Peyton was blessed with a great sense of discernment and wisdom. She knew Kelly needed her insight. "I know today was a major anniversary of a day in your life you'd like to forget, but...I have some exciting news for you!"

"Thanks for checking in on me. I guess I'm alright. And per usual, thank you my dear friend for reminding me of that dumpster fire of a day. But okay, what's your news?"

"As you know, this March was the 20-year anniversary of our Final Four appearance. The community wants to honor us with a special event this summer. You should come back. We would all love to see you!"

Pausing, Kelly sighed, then responded, "I don't know, Peyton."

"Oh, c'mon. Why not?" Peyton asked.

"This has just been a rough year, and I don't know if I'm in the right place mentally. I'm not sure I'd be much fun to be around."

"KJ, first and foremost you are not a failure," Peyton quipped back. "Secondly, I did not call you to talk to sad Kelly. So, pick up your chin, and get your head up! I know this season has been difficult for you, but the thing is you were made to rise above all of this."

Kelly felt her eyes begin to well with tears.

As Peyton could sense Kelly's pain, she continued. "Once a warrior, always a warrior. You have to always remember that, KJ. There isn't anything in this world you can't do. The good Lord put that in us."

Choking back tears, Kelly mustered out "I know."

Peyton continued, "Do you, though? Think about it. We need to see you, and I think you know you need to see your teammates. You know I'm right, and I won't take no for an answer, so get your plane ticket, book your hotel room at the 'ole Albany Inn, and I'll see you on June 19th! Love ya. You're going to be okay. I promise you. Remember, warriors rise to overcome together. TOTS!"

"Love ya, too, Peyton. Thank you again for checking up on me. I'll hopefully see you soon. Oh, TOTS!," Kelly giggled. "See ya, Peyton."

TOTS was their signature phrase as a team. After a game during their sophomore year of high school, the two friends were looking at a stat sheet with their teammates.

One of the freshman girls grabbed the stat sheet and said, "Wow, KJ, you had 20 tots?! That's awesome! But...what's a tot?"

Confused, Kelly gave the teammate a look and replied, "Tots?! Like a potato?"

Everyone laughed. The teammate shoved the stat sheet in Kelly's face, pointed at the stat line she was referring to, and said, "No, KJ! TOTS!"

Kelly picked up the statistic sheet. She placed her finger on the TOT line to discover what the teammate really meant. She laughed and replied, "Oh, you mean rebounds."

The girls all laughed as Kelly explained to the teammate, TOT stood for total rebounds. It was the term of endearment Peyton and KJ would say to each other on the court, especially in tense situations. It became a team joke for many years and actually became a phrase Kelly used frequently to describe total rebounds with the teams she coached. "Get me those TOTS," she often encouraged her players to do.

Kelly grabbed her basketball gear and headed home to arrange travel plans for her trip to her hometown. She grinned ear to ear, recalling the happy memories of basketball. Perhaps Peyton had a point. She needed to return home, to be reminded of the significance of being a warrior. As she walked to her car, Peyton's words echoed in her mind: "Warriors rise to overcome together."

4

BREAKDOWN

It was unusual for Kelly to be alert and active before 9:00 a.m. on a Saturday, but she found herself wide awake. She struggled to fall asleep at a decent time the night before, as she was completing all of her travel plans for her trip to Missouri. Kelly was never a morning person, but today she felt an overwhelming urge to get in an early workout. The basketball court she discovered in the park last month became her new mecca of relaxation and stress relief. She went every day since she found it. It was a place of solitude, with very little traffic. She cherished having this space to herself.

As she neared the blacktop, she noticed today she was not alone. A young woman was already shooting baskets. The young woman did not notice Kelly approaching the court, her hoodie pulled up and earbuds securely in place. Kelly did not want to disturb the young woman, so she headed to the other end of the court and stretched.

While she sat on the asphalt stretching her legs, she noticed the young woman suddenly bend over, place her hands on her knees, and tremble. Kelly observed her body language closely before deciding to approach. Her concern grew, but she hesitated, doubting her ability to assist someone in distress.

"Great. I'm the last person to try to provide this young lady any type of comfort," she whispered to herself. But her caring heart overruled her head.

As Kelly got up from stretching and began her swift walk to the other end of the court, the young woman collapsed to her knees and threw her face into her hands. She appeared to be sobbing. Kelly's swift walk quickly turned into a run. She approached the young woman, put her hand on her shoulder, and softly said, "I'm sorry to bother you, but I saw you collapse. Are you okay? Can I help?"

The young lady lifted her

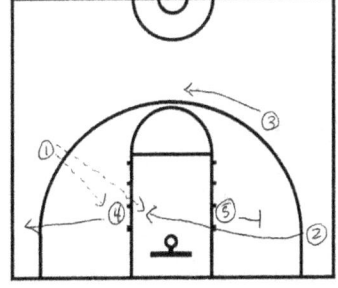

head and looked directly in Kelly's eyes. Immediately, Kelly recognized her face.

"Coach..." the young woman cried.

"Grace?!" Kelly exclaimed. "Oh, my goodness, are you okay? What's going on? What's wrong?"

Grace threw her arms around Kelly and wept uncontrollably.

Grace Villanueva was one of Kelly's former players. She was a talented guard, with an off-the-charts basketball IQ. Grace had a tremendous fire about her. And although they at times butted heads on the court, Kelly appreciated how passionate and reliable she was as a player. Grace was never afraid to meet Kelly face-to-face if she had any issues or questions about Kelly's decisions on the court, but she was always respectful. Kelly appreciated Grace kept an open line of communication. This was something, at times, lacking with other players.

Grace excelled both on the court and in the classroom. She was a natural leader and the type of student-athlete to successfully lead a team culture. Grace reminded Kelly of herself; she was like a protégé to her. Grace was often misunderstood by teammates because of some of her fiery antics on the court, but Kelly understood her desire to win. Kelly found it easy to coach Grace because they shared the same vision of how the game should be played. Grace was an emotional player with a flair for conducting exciting plays, an ability she learned from growing up playing against boys on the playground. She scored with ease and was a tremendous defender who had a knack for knowing where the ball came off the rim. She was a disciplined player, but she sometimes would go off script in games. It didn't bother Kelly because she wanted her players to be free when they played. However, not all of the players understood Grace or why Coach Janssen gave her a green light to execute her unique style on the court.

Despite being D-1 material, Grace was overlooked. Unfortunately, Grace's high school basketball experience weakened her confidence. This led to her sour attitude and self-doubt. Grace's talent was undeniable, but many of the college coaches recruiting her disliked her attitude on the court. Kelly saw her differently. On Kelly's first scouting trip, she recognized Grace as a diamond in the rough. They had an immediate connection, like their basketball souls had known each other forever. Coach Janssen earned Grace's trust, unlike her previous coaches. Grace knew Coach Janssen believed in her and saw her rising potential.

Grace was devastated when her beloved coach was fired. The idea of playing for another coach was unfathomable. Coach Janssen advised Grace to persevere and keep playing, but she struggled connecting with the new coach and maintaining connection with her teammates. New players did not see eye-to-eye with Grace's style of play—neither did the new coach. She was pressing, yet hoped the connection would manifest on the court. The more Grace wanted to play well, the worse she played. She could not find her rhythm, and she felt the weight of the team on her shoulders.

The green light Grace once had to be herself on the court was extinguished. Anytime she did not follow the game plan or made a razzle-dazzle play, she would get benched—sometimes for the remainder of the game. Her minutes started getting cut. Her confidence shattered. At this stage of her college career, she felt as though she had taken ten steps back as a player.

She was ostracized by the team. Whispers in the locker room suggested she had become the scapegoat for the team's struggles. At that moment, she experienced a profound sense of loneliness among her teammates. This season, marred by ongoing injuries, felt distinctly different for her.

Grace was a prime example of the players Kelly sought—overlooked, talented kids lacking in self-confidence due to negative past experiences. So many times, Kelly would find an overlooked player other college coaches or even their own high school coaches would advise her not to waste her time recruiting.

"You don't want that kid!" was usually an indication to Kelly to recruit that player.

It was a mystery to Kelly, but her mission was to find those specific players. Kelly found herself called to take what others deemed as broken misfits and guide them to become whole again. She relished the opportunity to build them up. She had a desire to nurture them to find their purpose. Kelly felt like God gave her a gift to see something in these young women others could not see. Years prior to coaching, Kelly stumbled upon a quote by Ayesha Siddiqi who simply stated, "Be the person you needed when you were younger." This became her personal creed.

It was months since Kelly last saw Grace. Kelly wanted to support her former players, but she could not bring herself to attend any games. She was embarrassed to show her face. She knew her presence would put her former players in an awkward position with their new coaches. It was also difficult for her to even imagine someone else coaching her girls, and she felt she would be a distraction. Even though Grace understood why Kelly chose not to attend games, she also felt a sense of abandonment from her former coach. Coach Janssen was Grace's pillar of strength on the court. Without Coach on the sideline, she wasn't herself. With the season and her basketball career unraveling, Grace felt more alone than ever.

As Grace continued to cry into her shoulder, Kelly could feel the weight of Grace's anguish transferring into her own spirit. Kelly again found herself flashing back to her own painful memories. As she remembered a moment in junior high, she found it difficult to focus on what was happening with Grace.

Flashback: Spring 1996

It was a cloudy day in the spring of 1996. Kelly arrived home from school. Her mom was in bed, which was nothing new. She tried to wake her mom up, saying she was home, but her mom mumbled a few words and fell back asleep. Kelly, frustrated, headed to the outdoor basketball court near her house and shot some hoops to de-stress. She wanted to share with her mom some exciting news from school, but like most days, Anne seemed to not care.

As a young teen, Kelly did not recognize the symptoms of

depression, and grew angry with her mom for her behavior. She knew deep down it was not her mom's fault, but she was not old enough to fully understand her mom's situation. On really bad days, everything seemed to be Kelly's fault.

After shooting at the court for about an hour, Kelly began to worry about Anne's incoherence when she told her she was going to the basketball court. She worried her dad wouldn't know where she was when he arrived home from work. It had been a grim year already, as the family continued to grieve over the death of Grandma Elaine, who introduced basketball to her. The last thing she wanted to do was to cause any additional stress for her parents.

When Kelly arrived home, the house was locked. Her dad's car was not in the driveway. Kelly found a way into the house from the basement, went upstairs to find her mom, and realized nobody was home. Frantically searching the house, Kelly panicked. An instant state of fear swept through her body something bad had happened. She was now seriously worried. As she ran downstairs, Axel swung open the front door and yelled, "Where have you been?!"

"I was at the basketball court," Kelly sheepishly responded.

"Grab your stuff!" her dad yelled. "We have to go to the hospital!"

As Kelly's mind raced and wandered, something snapped her back to the present day.

Grace lifted her head from Kelly's shoulder and said, "Coach, I don't know what to do."

5

GRACE

Grace dealt with tragedy after tragedy in her 21 years of life. She knew the tragedies she experienced molded her into who she was today. She made every effort not to allow those experiences to affect how she lives now. A usually out-spoken, upbeat individual, she cared about academics and performing well on the basketball court. She mostly kept to herself, but was friendly to everyone. She had many acquaintances, but few close friends.

Grace's parents divorced when she was a young child. It was an ugly divorce; negatively affecting her and her older brother, Trey. Grace's father wanted nothing to do with her because she reminded him too much of her mother; Grace's mother was heartbroken over her divorce and bitter towards Grace's father. Her mother began drinking heavily and struggling with keeping a job to support her children. Her mother also dealt with health issues which required constant care her family could not provide. All of this led to Grace and Trey living with their grandmother who they lovingly called Nana.

Ten years older than Grace, Trey often acted as the father she needed. Trey was an all-star basketball player, an amazing talent, incredibly handsome, and the ultimate boy next door. Some of the leading D-1 universities in the nation recruited him. Trey taught the game of basketball to Grace, and it was something that created a strong bond between them. He became her rock. As strong as Trey was for Grace, he struggled with depression, too. When Trey broke his ankle in a high school basketball game, his injury led to an addiction to prescription drugs. This combined with his depression marked the beginning of his life spiraling out of control. He lost all his D-1 college offers and settled on playing basketball at a junior college. He eventually dropped out. He was in and out of rehabilitation centers and couldn't maintain a steady job.

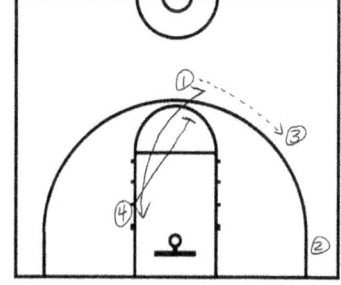

Grace tried to keep Trey above water. Only she could get

through to him, she felt. When Trey could no longer overcome his inner pain, he took his own life when Grace was a sophomore in high school. His death affected her in ways she never would have imagined, but she knew she had to keep living for her brother. She wore the number three, his jersey number, as her jersey number from that point forward.

After Trey died, Nana became Grace's support system, and they grew closer during her high school career. Nana was Grace's number one fan—sitting in the stands at games proudly wearing a "#3's GRANDMA" T-shirt. Nana wore it to every basketball game she attended through Grace's high school and college career.

Similar to Coach Janssen, Grace turned to basketball to deal with her grief. Although she had a positive and outgoing personality, she truly felt like no one understood her and what she was going through. Frankly, only her brother did, and he was gone. When she had a basketball in her hand, she felt connected to Trey. And when she put on the #3 jersey, she felt him with her.

Grace never talked about her family life with anyone. She did not want people to feel sorry for her. She never wanted to use any of her past as a crutch or as an excuse. Because of her family's dysfunctional dynamics, she found it challenging to open up to her peers and teammates. When teammates and others shared stories of their family events, she kept quiet as she could not relate. Her family wasn't like the families of her teammates. She was embarrassed and assumed they would ostracize her more if they knew the truth of the difficulties she faced through her young life. As challenging as life was, she kept her optimism these life experiences would make her a stronger and a more resilient person.

Coach Janssen gave Grace a sense of safety and trust. Although she was her coach, Grace looked at Coach Janssen more as Kelly, a big sister figure. She reminded Grace a lot of Trey. Kelly and Trey were close in age and both had the same passion and philosophies about basketball. Kelly's personality was quite similar, too. She was kind and had a huge heart, sometimes to her own downfall. Grace believed if Trey was still alive, Kelly would have been his ideal soulmate. As she got to know Kelly better, she often wondered if Trey would have met Kelly in high school or college, maybe she would have been the one to save him. So, as Grace started her freshman year in college, she began opening up little by little to Coach Janssen about her life, her tragedies, her dreams and goals, and everything in-between. She never shared how much Coach reminded her of Trey, though she talked about Trey frequently. Coach Janssen was the only one at the university who truly knew Grace's story.

Grace's outlook for a successful junior basketball season was quickly diminished as her personal life took a toll on her preseason play and in the classroom. The university fired Coach Janssen the previous spring, and her grandmother was in the early stages of showing signs of illness. She moved out of the dorms after her sophomore year to live with Nana. Her grandmother received a lung cancer diagnosis in October, as the basketball season began. Grace was already balancing academics, basketball and work. Getting Nana to chemotherapy and doctor appointments on top of her busy schedule became overwhelming. She had to be strong for her grandmother, so she never told her she felt like she was drowning.

The few friends Grace had at school left college for various reasons before her junior year. Grace was normally a high-achieving student but began struggling in the classroom. With Coach Janssen no longer there pushing her to present her best academic self, she began falling behind, failing tests, and having uncharacteristic behavioral issues with her professors.

After months of battling cancer, Nana died. Grace told no one Nana had died.

Not her professors.
Not her coaches.
Not her teammates.
No one knew,
SHE WAS ALONE.

She had already withdrawn herself from the team. No longer

living on campus and only being there for class and basketball activities withdrew her further. After she suffered her season-ending injury, she stopped showing up to basketball altogether. Many of her teammates assumed her disappearance was because she was disinterested in being a part of the team. They considered her actions selfish and stopped inviting her and involving her with team activities. They did not know the private war she was fighting alone. Her reclusiveness resulted from depression.

Nana died on April 19. Following Nana's cremation, the family held her funeral on May 19. Grace never felt more alone in the world. She once again felt abandoned. The only three people in her life she trusted were gone.

Grace grew up Catholic, but she would never classify herself as a religious individual. Nana had a heart for the Lord and would make her go to mass every so often, but Grace found the rules, rituals, and traditions of the Catholic church to be exhausting and difficult to understand. She would only attend for Nana. Coach Janssen would often share her beliefs in Jesus with Grace, giving her an avenue to ask questions and talk about faith. Yet, Grace remained unsure about her belief in God.

After the funeral, she drove around town trying to find a basketball court. Basketball was the only thing she could still hold onto. It was her therapy. She spotted a community park, and there it was—a glorious blacktop court. There was nothing special about this court, but Grace felt immediate peace the minute she got out of her car. She was surprised she had never found this secluded court before. No one else was around, and she felt like she could finally let out all of her emotions.

Grace felt cold, so she threw on her hoodie, popped in her earbuds, and started shooting. The more she shot, the more she felt all the years of anger, sadness and confusion poured out onto the court. Questions consumed her. Why were the only people she ever felt safe and close to taken away? How was she ever going to make it in this world now? Exhausted and beaten down, she collapsed to her knees upon the court. For the first time in her life, she prayed.

"God, I don't know how to do this. I don't know if you are real or even care, but I can't do any of my life alone. Please help me," Grace cried out. She was unsure she was praying the correct way.

As she was on her knees wailing, she suddenly felt a hand on her shoulder and heard a voice. It startled her because she did not hear or see anyone in the vicinity and thought maybe God was coming to strike her down. As she looked up, she could not clearly make out the figure as the sun above was radiating beams into her eyes. Then, as the figure leaned down and blocked the direct light, she recognized the comforting face.

6

LOSING STREAK

Kelly recognized Grace was a mess and would not open up about it. Kelly was concerned about Grace's breakdown and wondered what led to this and why she would not confide in her what was going on. Kelly left the court after the encounter with Grace, distraught.

"Who am I kidding?" Kelly thought as she started her car. "I can't even help myself. Why would Grace ever listen to me when all I did was let her down?"

As Kelly drove away, the anger poured out of her.

"WHY GOD?"
SHE YELLED, LOOKING UP IN THE AIR.

"Stop putting me in these situations! You took basketball away from me, so why are you putting me in this situation? I obviously can't help her. You made that incredibly clear the day you took everything I loved away from me."

She punched the steering wheel and let out a scream of frustration. Just when she thought she was moving on, something would trigger her and pull her back into a state of psychological devastation and despair. In basketball terms, it was like she was in a never ending losing streak. Her mental health was in a terrible state. She didn't want to admit to herself she was consumed by dangerous behaviors because she knew she would have to be accountable for them. The destructive path she propelled herself into the past year was driven by her depression and grief. Her thoughts were irrational, and her behavior followed suit.

When Kelly was coaching, she had a regular workout routine, but going to the gym or doing anything exercise-related reminded her of basketball, so she stopped. She had only recently picked up

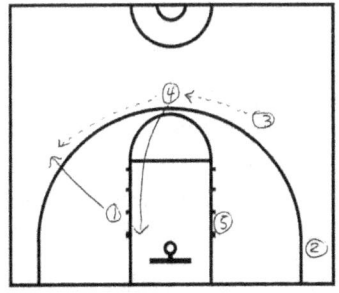

a basketball in an attempt to find her old self once again. The past year she sought comfort and satisfaction in worldly pleasures; binge drinking alcohol, engaging in temporary relationships with toxic men, indulging in unhealthy food, and wasting money on material possessions. She wanted to disassociate from all the emotions, thoughts, and memories which invaded her mind. Instead of turning to Jesus, she turned to the world. It was uncharacteristic of her to act this way. She knew she was falling, but she failed at stopping herself. Every time she began to pull herself out of self-destruction, she spiraled again.

Driving around like a maniac, Kelly suddenly drove at high speeds on back country roads. She did not know where she was, nor did she care.

"It would be a shame if I wrecked! Like you care! Like anyone would care!" she yelled.

Trembling, the tears began streaming down her face. As she took the upcoming curve too fast, a deer suddenly appeared in the lane ahead of her. She slammed on her brakes and hit her horn. Luckily, the deer turned around and headed back into the wooded area off the road before Kelly's car came to a complete stop. She took in a deep breath, then began sobbing and hyperventilating. She did not really want to die.

Kelly turned on the navigation on her phone to try to find her way home. She questioned everything she always believed. Even with all the hardships she went through growing up, she never once lost her faith in God even if it was at times only the size of a mustard seed. But now, she struggled to understand why God would bring her what she thought was her purpose, only to take it from her. She tried to be an example and a light to her players. Maybe she should have been more outspoken about her faith. She was worried she would say the wrong thing, offend someone, and get fired for it. Deep down, she felt like she wasn't living out what she claimed to believe. It didn't matter now. Somewhere during her coaching stint, Kelly realized she lost herself. She wanted to cry out to God for help, but she was ashamed. The battle in her mind raged on.

Tears filled her eyes to where she could barely see as she entered a small town. She pulled her car into an empty parking lot and continued crying. The parking lot reminded her of the first time she went to an open gym when she started coaching. She replayed past conversations, including one with the first player she ever met at the first open gym - her former player, Maya.

Maya transferred into the program during Kelly's first year of coaching. She graduated a couple years prior and would attend games periodically to support her former coach and the team. Like Grace, Kelly experienced an immediate connection with Maya the first time they met. Maya was a reliable, undersized forward who played larger than her stature. Her bubbly personality and her laugh were contagious. She was outspoken and sometimes a bit too blunt. However, her heart was pure. She had a presence about her that lit up a room. Kelly loved when former players came to games, so she was excited to catch up with her.

As Coach Janssen and Maya began talking, current players were leaving the gym. Kelly tried to make sure she stopped each player to reassure them with some sort of positive comment as they left. It was another tough loss in a game they had every chance to win. They were not ready to play, and Kelly could not understand why. It was a trend happening too often over the past few games. Maya smiled, but continued on talking about her current job situation and other things going on in her life.

Out of the corner of her eye, Kelly noticed a player who had a terrible game slip out of the locker room. Kelly excused herself from her conversation with Maya to offer the player a quick word of encouragement. The player looked down at her shoes, nodded, and left without saying a word. Kelly walked back over to Maya and apologized for stepping away and interrupting their conversation. Then, Maya's statement took Kelly completely off guard, as she hadn't expected it.

"You've changed as a coach," Maya said.

"What?" Kelly replied. "What do you mean by that?"

"C'mon, Coach. You wouldn't have let us get away with some of the things you seem to be letting this team get away with," Maya responded. "I'm just a little surprised you aren't coaching them harder."

"What are you talking about, Maya?" Kelly snapped back. She was already frustrated with how her team played, and the last thing she wanted to hear was criticism. "You know, I appreciate your support, but you aren't around the team anymore. So, I don't know where you get off making a statement like that."

"Look, I don't mean to make you mad, Coach, but you never would have acted this way with me. I don't know. You just don't seem to be the same coach I had," Maya retorted.

"O-kay…" Kelly clapped back sarcastically.

"You really can't see it, can you? Those players have no respect for you," Maya replied.

"That's a pretty bold statement from an outsider. How am I not the same coach, exactly, Maya!" Kelly said as she raised her voice in frustration.

"Well, I think this conversation is a perfect example," Maya said. "You were never afraid to call me out, like you are right now. I just watched you coddle each and every one of those players as they left the gym. They don't need coddling, Coach. They need tough love. This loss was on them, and you are acting like they did nothing wrong. Hold them accountable. Stop making excuses for them. They need to grow up. You aren't the coach I knew."

Kelly was irritated by this point. She decided to end the conversation before she said something she would regret. She did not have time for this, and this conversation seemed out of left field. "Well, Maya, it was great to see you, too. I've got to go. Have a good evening."

She grabbed her things and left the gym angry. She could not believe after everything she did for Maya during her playing days, Maya had the audacity to say what she said. Kelly was offended and in no mood to pick a fight. Maya sent several texts to apologize for how she had approached Kelly. She followed up with words of encouragement, reminding Kelly of the kind of coach she was and urging her not to let the players dictate how she coached. Kelly ignored all of her texts. She was so enraged, and she didn't want to entertain this conversation any longer.

As Kelly sat in the parking lot recalling that conversation, she thought maybe Maya was right. She now realized what Maya was trying to convey to her. Kelly coached with passion her first couple of years. She coached the way she wanted to be coached - stern, but loving. She held players accountable, and they wanted to follow and do their best. With each passing year, she started listening to advice on how to coach from other seasoned professionals. Instead of balancing the advice with her own style, she realized she lost the coach she wanted to be. Kelly wondered when the turning point was. When did she lose the team? Most importantly, when did she really lose herself?

Kelly thought about her trip home for the high school reunion. Going was not something she wanted to do. Emotionally, she was completely depleted. She was mentally in a terrible place. The last thing she wanted to do was to go home a loser.

Despite cherishing her time in Albany, she perpetually grappled with self-doubt and undervalued her achievements. Though skilled and talented, she was never the top athlete or the smartest student, fueling a relentless need to prove herself. She yearned to demonstrate her worthiness, seeing a career as a college coach as her chance to finally feel adequate and suppress all of her internal insecurities. However, losing her job left her feeling like a disappointment.

"I've literally done nothing with my life," she said to herself. "I have no one. I've been so consumed by my career, and I don't even have that anymore. Same ol' Kelly. Just never good enough."

Her mind was a constant battlefield of survival. She felt no hope, and she was terrified. She did not even want to admit to herself she was having these types of thoughts. Her mother struggled with mental health for years, and Kelly was afraid she was now headed down the same path. She didn't know how she could ever get out of this dark depression and truly live again.

7

HOME

The months flew by, and Kelly could not believe the time had arrived for her to travel home. She was excited yet anxious. It was well over 10 years since she was last in her hometown. As she waited at the gate for her flight to board, she got a text from Peyton:

```
Can't wait to see you! Let me know when you land!
```

During her flight, Kelly only thought of Grace. It had been a month since she witnessed Grace's breakdown at the blacktop court. Kelly tried to contact her, to no avail. She sent text messages, left voicemails, and even mailed her a "thinking of you" card, but Grace seemed to ignore all of her efforts. Grace never really said what made her collapse, but Kelly became concerned it was Grace's grandmother, Nana.

Nana was a sweet, positive woman with a lot of passion. Grace had many of Nana's personality attributes, including her innate kindness. Kelly appreciated everything Nana did for the team, including baking cookies and making treats for away games. But what meant the most was how Nana would find Kelly after every game, give her a hug, and tell her, "You keep working hard with those girls. You don't know the impact you are making." As a coach, it always meant a great deal to her when Nana took the time to offer such heartfelt words, especially given the criticism she received from a few negative parents.

As Kelly's mind wandered, she thought about Nana and Grace. She had an overwhelming feeling she needed to keep praying and trying to contact Grace. She could not explain it, but a feeling in the pit of her stomach made her believe something bad happened.

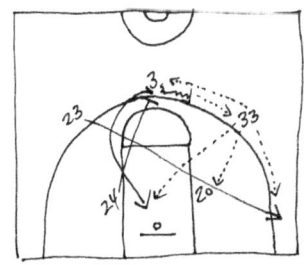

From the first day she met Grace, Kelly believed their lives crossed paths for a significant reason. During the years of coaching Grace, Kelly felt as though someone whispered to her soul, "Guide her. There's a plan." Obviously, a lot had happened over the past year which redirected her feelings. She began hearing a faint voice again. As she settled into her flight, she silently prayed.

The two-hour drive to her hometown from the airport went surprisingly fast. Kelly thought of all the long bus rides to games, traveling to her summer league games and tournaments with her teammates, or enduring those long drives home with her parents. This trip was already reminding her that sometimes you have to remember where you came from to move forward. As she pulled into town, she saw an uplifting landmark.

Twenty years ago, as her team made their playoff run to state, a thunderstorm rolled through their town and lightning struck a tree. The tree fell to the shape of the letter "A." The timing had to be fate. Everyone in the town of 2,000 people viewed it as a good omen for the girls' basketball team, and it proved to be. The team made a run which no other team had made. Kelly smiled, driving by the symbolic "A." She needed this trip home.

The high school had changed little since Kelly graduated 20 years ago. It was a surreal feeling as she walked into the commons area outside of the gym. It felt like stepping back in time. She smiled as she passed by the trophy case proudly displaying her team's third place finish at the state tournament.

As she approached the entrance of the gym, she heard a few familiar voices call her name. Most of her teammates made the trip back to their hometown to celebrate. They were genuinely happy to see her. However, Kelly still felt an overwhelming amount of apprehension about her coaching situation. Admittingly, she was still very embarrassed about getting fired, and she dreaded being asked this question.

"Hey, KJ," Peyton said as she walked up and gave Kelly one of the tightest hugs she had ever received in her life.

Peyton said little else at the moment. She just smiled and

ushered Kelly and the others into the gym. As they sat in the stands and waited for the ceremony, they shared funny team stories from all the years they played together. For the first time in months, Kelly finally relaxed and forgot about all her pain.

As they sat waiting for the ceremony, Peyton slid over on the bleachers, closer to Kelly. "Are you going to coach this year?" she asked quietly.

"I don't know," Kelly responded.

"Why not? I think you should. You obviously loved it, and you obviously miss it," Peyton said.

"And I obviously sucked at it," Kelly replied. "I don't know what I'm supposed to do, Peyton. Maybe that's why God took it away from me."

Peyton smiled with a laugh, "KJ...God didn't take coaching away from you. That's what you think? Stop with this pity party you are throwing for yourself. This isn't you. Do you honestly think God stole basketball from you? No way! If anything, I think he's going to redeem you. This is nothing but a blessing."

The look of disgust was written all over Kelly's face. Trying to keep her voice down and not disrupt everyone around them, Kelly snapped back, "Are you serious? A blessing. Really? That's a joke!"

"No, this isn't a joke, KJ." Peyton looked directly into Kelly's eyes. "I'm being serious. I can't explain it, but I just believe in my gut God's saving you. We may never fully know why any of this happened. But what I do believe is He is using this. So yes, it is a blessing. In fact, I now know why." Peyton grinned and slid back over to where she was originally sitting on the bleachers.

Kelly was confused about what in the world Peyton was even talking about. Peyton continued to smile, glancing over at Kelly often. "Why are you being so weird?" Kelly said to Peyton.

"You'll see," Peyton said. Peyton continued smiling while the team took the court to be recognized by the town.

The ceremony and experience of being back home surrounded by her former teammates, coaches and community was a big step. It helped remind Kelly of who she was and what she had overcome. The rest of the weekend seemed to fly by. Kelly enjoyed many laughs and precious time with her former team. It was just what she needed, but it was now time to say goodbye.

Peyton grabbed Kelly's arm and said, "Hey, let's chat before you leave." The two teammates headed outside near Kelly's rental car.

"I'm really glad you came, KJ. You needed this. It seemed like you were having a great time, which was definitely the goal. But I have to be honest, I get the sense you are still not okay."

"Well, I'm still trying to figure out what in the world you were talking about in the gym. I felt like I was doing okay until about a month ago when I ran into a former player at this outdoor court I've been going to," Kelly explained. "She's a great kid. She's dealt with so much tragedy in her young life. I just don't know how I can help her. Since the moment I met her, I've just always felt this need to help her. But, I'm not in a good place myself right now, so how am I supposed to help this broken kid? She's experienced so much loss, and I can tell she's dealing with something else. She won't talk to me since I last saw her. I've tried to just let things play out, but honestly, I'm really worried about her."

"I'll definitely keep her in my prayers," Peyton said. "KJ, I think you underestimate yourself. I know you love helping people, and I completely believe God gifted you with this ability to be a light for others. But...you also have to remember, as hard as this is to say, you can't save them all."

"But I can try. And I've got to try with this kid. I cannot explain why, but I must try," Kelly said in a somber tone.

Kelly's empathy was one of her greatest strengths, yet also one of her deepest burdens. This was what made things so difficult for Kelly when she coached. She sometimes cared too much, and the responsibility she placed on herself was more than she could manage. She wondered why she always had a compelling urge to save others. This behavior was, in some ways, contributing to her ultimate downfall. While it was a wonderful character trait, it was also her greatest flaw.

"You know what your name means, right?" asked Peyton.

"What? Where do you pull these thoughts from, Peyton? And what does my name have to do with anything?" Kelly was already feeling a little on edge and agitated just thinking about not being able to help Grace.

Peyton laughed. "What does it have to do with anything?! Kelly, it has literally everything to do with this. For goodness' sake, your name means WARRIOR. It means this is bigger than you, KJ. Life is a constant battle of good versus evil. God put that warrior spirit in you for a reason. He knew you were going to go through these difficult times, and He also knew you were going to be tasked with fighting for others. Your experiences were to prepare you to mentor those He places in your care. You were blessed with the gift of empathy. You are here to be the voice for the voiceless. You are here to battle for those who are too weak to fight for themselves. It honestly makes a lot of sense to me."

Kelly sighed.

"Kelly, the way I see it you are at a crossroads. It's your choice of how you are going to handle this adversity. You can choose to be a loser - be negative all the time, blame everyone else, just give up, never try again, and proceed without God. Or, you can choose the other path to victory. You can rise up, believe in yourself because of your confidence in who you are in Jesus, learn from this loss, and embrace failure knowing it is the thing that is going to make you great. The Kelly Janssen I know is a champion for Christ. You just lost your spark for a minute, friend. Now go find it and rise back up with the fire I know you have for people and this game!"

Deep down, Kelly knew Peyton was right, but she was still struggling with how she could move on.

"Thanks, Peyton. Even though you are super annoying at times, you're such a great friend."

The friends laughed and then hugged, and Kelly opened her rental car door to leave for the airport. Kelly shut the car door and put the car into drive when she heard Peyton yelling and banging on the side of her rental car. Kelly rolled down her window.

"Wait," Peyton exclaimed. "I have something for you." Peyton pulled out of her back pocket a small journal and handed it to Kelly. "I want you to have this. Read it on your flight home. Remember, the greatest comebacks are a process. Be patient. Get those TOTS, my friend. I love you," Peyton smiled, and Kelly smiled back.

"TOTS," Kelly chuckled. "I love you, too, Peyton."

The two-hour drive to the airport seemed much longer than the trip to Albany. Kelly's mind toggled back and forth about what Peyton said in ways she could help Grace. As she boarded her plane, she found her seat next to the window. Kelly pulled the journal out of her carry-on bag. There was an old piece of athletic tape stuck on the front of the book with the title *"The R.I.S.E. Playbook"* written with what looked like a black Sharpie. Kelly giggled because she labeled her totes of basketball equipment and other things at home with athletic tape. It was clear someone spent a lot of time on this playbook. It was aged and worn, exhibiting the wear of countless reads. As Kelly opened the book, she noticed a special message from Peyton written on a separate piece of paper that was folded and tucked into the playbook.

Dear Kelly,

I'm so blessed to call you my friend and teammate. I know recently life has thrown some junk defenses at you that have thrown you off your game plan. It's incredibly rare to go undefeated in basketball. You don't go undefeated in this life. We all will face some sort of adversity. Ultimately, it is up to you to decide whether you are going to let adversity define you or refine you. No one wants to go through difficult and challenging times, but I firmly believe God will turn the bad into good. The adversity may actually be the turning point in your life that propels you to your purpose.

I have gone through my own seasons of pain. A win in life might be just getting out of bed each day, and that's okay. It's okay to grieve. It's okay to feel sadness. It's okay to cry. It's okay to be angry. If you are clutching onto your faith that's only the size of a mustard seed, it's all you need. It's okay to just do your best to survive and advance right now. And when you can't, allow Jesus to carry you. God did not create us to walk this Earth alone and to try to figure everything out based on our own understanding. Our plans fail. His plans prevail.

Remember, even the prophet Elijah experienced depression. What did God do for Elijah while he was experiencing these feelings of hopelessness, sadness, and wanting to die? He gave him rest. Jesus says, "Come to me all who are weary and burdened, and I will give you rest." - Matthew 11:28 (NIV) In other words, it's okay to take a timeout to rest, refresh, and refocus, and let Jesus metaphorically take the wheel. Jesus understands what you are going through as a human being. He was mocked by the world, betrayed and denied by his friends, and misunderstood by many. He's here to carry you through all of the storms of life.

I thought you might need a new playbook to help guide you to your purpose. Remember, this is a team sport. We don't win alone. We overcome and win together. Rely on your "teammates." Trust your training and your ability. Trust "Coach's" game plan. Remember, you can't come back from a 20-point deficit with a single shot. Comebacks are a process. There will be setbacks. It may be painful at times but it will be worth it. Sometimes you just have to take a timeout, and that is okay. Survive and advance. Keep a champion's mentality. We always walk on the court expecting to win. You've got this!

You are a Warrior, you know, and

WARRIORS RISE!

Love, Peyton

8

WARRIOR

T he trip to her hometown was exactly the identity reminder Kelly needed, but she was happy to be back on the East Coast and her routine. She felt a renewed spirit in her soul. She read through *The R.I.S.E. Playbook* repeatedly during the two-and-a-half-hour flight home. The words of wisdom shared in the playbook resonated with Kelly. The playbook principles were accompanied by special messages from Peyton, stories and reminders she knew Kelly would need. Kelly hoped the playbook would help her heal and ultimately help others.

Kelly was surprised she was not jet lagged the next morning after arriving home so late. For the first time in over a year, she had a full night of sleep. Her mind no longer felt tormented. She woke up refreshed.

As she took her time getting ready for the day, the meaning of her name, Kelly, continued to run through her mind. The term "warrior" was such a common word in her vocabulary growing up. Why didn't she realize what her name meant? Maybe she knew the significance, yet it seems more relevant now. It was her high school team's mascot. It was part of a special scripture her mom shared with her as a child to help Kelly conquer her fears.

Kelly read Jeremiah 20:11 aloud. "But the LORD is with me like a mighty warrior; so my persecutors will stumble and not prevail. They will fail and be thoroughly disgraced; their dishonor will never be forgotten." Even though she was still angry at God, she tried to stay connected by reading the Bible daily.

She decided she was going to go to the blacktop basketball court later in the morning. She had consistently gone for two months before her trip to Missouri. The basketball therapy sessions on the court helped her release her stress. She arrived at the court, stretched, and began her shooting routine.

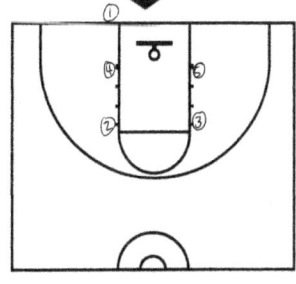

As she was casually shooting, she heard a voice behind her in the distance. "Coach?"

When Kelly turned around, she was stunned to see Grace.

"Grace...you're here! How are you doing?!" Kelly exclaimed. She ran toward her and gave her a hug.

Tears began to well up in Grace's eyes. "I don't know," Grace replied. Wiping away tears, she told Kelly Nana had cancer. She didn't say much else except how she was trying to just survive.

"Coach, I'm so sorry I haven't replied to you. I appreciate you checking in on me. I just didn't know how to respond."

"Grace, I get it. No worries," Kelly looked straight into Grace's eyes. "What can I do to help you?"

Grace shrugged her shoulders looking down at her feet. She then lifted her head, looked Kelly directly in the eyes, and said, "Would you train me?"

"Train you?" Kelly questioned. "Like basketball train you? I'm not the person who you need now, Grace."

"Yes and no, Coach," Grace responded. "Like...physical training and life training. Honestly, that's what I miss the most about you being my coach. You always shared these great life stories. I realized this last year why you shared those stories, and well...it's what I miss most."

Kelly stared at Grace, stunned. She always hoped some of her advice and words of wisdom were sinking into her players. Judging by their blank stares most often, Kelly figured the advice went in one ear and out the other. However, she hoped perhaps someday they would look back and think about things she shared. Coaching was more than just about the game of basketball for Kelly. She truly cared about her players, their goals, their achievements, and where they were headed in life. "Be the person you needed when you were younger" was the quote she lived by.

"Grace, I don't know I'm the best person to even do that," Kelly replied.

Grace looked down again at her shoes, then looked up at Kelly. "Coach, you know I saw you that day."

Kelly was confused about what Grace was referring to.

"What day?"

"The day you got fired. I saw you," Grace said.

"Yeah, I remember you being there," Kelly replied.

"No, Coach. I mean I saw you that day. I SAW you. You are always so confident and just seemed to have it all. I've never seen you broken. I realized when you get cut, you bleed, too. I guess you never think of your basketball coach that way."

Kelly choked back tears. "Grace, I don't have it all. I've never had it all. We all have a story."

"I know, Coach. But, we never saw that side of you," Grace said. "Actually, Coach, may I ask you a personal question?"

"Sure, Grace," Kelly replied.

"Why are you letting this coaching job define you? It doesn't and never did. Those who respect you and care about you need you back in their lives. I need you back," Grace took in a deep breath and sighed. "Nana died. The other coach doesn't even know. The team doesn't even know."

Kelly's intuition was spot on. She now knew why she had a horrible gut feeling about Grace. Grace had lost everyone she loved—she had every right to be sad, angry, and bitter towards the world. And yet, she has never used this as an excuse. Kelly wiped a tear from her cheek. Kelly locked eyes with Grace, "Oh, Grace. I'm so sorry. I didn't know you were dealing with this alone."

"It's okay," Grace said as she wiped a tear from her eye. "It's hard talking about it. I've just been walking around like a zombie, I guess. Would you please train me?"

"I can try," Kelly responded. She was hesitant, but she knew Grace just needed someone right now. But what advice could she possibly give, Kelly thought. She let her own brokenness get the best of her, and she just was not herself.

Kelly remembered what Peyton said to her about her name, meaning warrior. She was made to fight for those who cannot battle for themselves. Maybe this was the right time to take action.

"Grace, this may seem like the most random question ever, but what does your name mean?" Kelly asked.

"My name? Well, Nana's middle name was Grace," Grace choked back the lump in her throat. Tears streamed down her face. "So, I was named after her. Nana always said my name meant favor in God's eyes. I don't know what that means exactly, but it always made me feel good. I don't think that's very true though."

"Favor in God's eyes," Kelly smiled. "Of course, it does." It finally clicked. Kelly understood what she was supposed to do. It was not a mistake she met Grace. It was not a mistake she was reunited with her. Kelly knew she was supposed to guide and mentor her.

Was it fate Peyton gave Kelly this encouraging playbook? Perhaps this is what Peyton meant when she said she now knew why.

"A good friend of mine actually gave me something when I went home to Missouri this past weekend. I think you need this just as much as I do. I know we have both been through a lot, especially recently. I don't know about you, but I think it is time we rise up."

"Sounds great to me, Coach," Grace smiled back at her.

Kelly continued, "Basketball was always my way to cope, escape, and heal from things going on in my life when I was a kid. This past year has really made me realize you can't push all of those past experiences down into a dark abyss of your mind, hoping you will never deal with them again. It will resurface. For some reason, it was losing my coaching job that made everything resurface. I can't shut my brain off. All of those things I tried to forget about and deal with on my own came to the surface. God didn't create us to walk this Earth alone. I was trying to fight these battles on my own. And I realize, I can't. We all have a story, Grace. Although I probably haven't acted like this lately, I do believe deep down our own struggles will ultimately be used to help someone else. I cannot always understand what others are going through, but I can be compassionate and listen because there may be a piece of my past that is relatable. You have an incredible story, Grace. I believe you are at an impasse in your story that is going to make you or break you. Please don't be like me and let it break you. Let it make you into someone who can help someone else in the future."

"I guess we are more alike than I ever realized," Grace said.

"Yeah, we really are," said Kelly.

"You know, Coach, I think you are at the same impasse, and I think you need to listen to your own advice," Grace replied.

Kelly shook her head and responded, "Yeah, I guess maybe I do."

"By the way, Coach, what does your name mean?" Grace asked.

Kelly smirked, "Warrior."

"Perfect. A true warrior has the heart and perseverance to overcome any obstacle and rise above so they may come out successful and stronger than when they started. That's you!" Grace said proudly.

"Wow, Grace. How insightful," Kelly replied. "Where did you hear this from?"

"Well, our high school team was the Warriors, and it was a saying Trey had posted in his room."

Grace paused for a moment. Kelly noticed Grace's pause was most likely her mind was drifting to memories. Grace continued, "You would have really loved him, Coach. Actually, you are a lot like him. I know you have been very sad, but I also know you are strong and tough. You will rebound, and you will find something or somewhere that appreciates you. You are a warrior, you know."

Kelly reluctantly smiled back at Grace. She hoped it was true. "That's right. I forgot both our high school team mascots were the Warriors. Another commonality between us. Thanks, Grace."

Both continued their basketball workouts on opposite ends of the blacktop, but after about 15 minutes Kelly ended hers to rebound for Grace. Kelly could tell Grace had poured a lot of emotion into her shooting routine. She was drenched in sweat and breathing heavily. Grace always worked hard in practice, but this was another level of intensity Kelly had not seen in her.

"I'm going to head home, Grace," Kelly said after about an hour. "I'll see you next week for training. How about Sunday morning?"

Grabbing the ball out of the net, Grace replied, "Really? Yes,

Coach. Oh, I'll be here for basketball church." She winked at Kelly and kept shooting.

9

RELEASE

Sunday mornings were the perfect day to heal in Kelly's mind. Basketball church was now in session, as Grace would say. Kelly arrived at the court early on this first Sunday morning with a renewed spirit. She felt like her sense of purpose was reignited. She brought a portable speaker from home and began playing music while she was stretching. It was common for Coach Janssen to play music often during practices, and she needed the music to get herself going.

Kelly's high school coach would preach, "if you are early, you are on time. If you are on time, you are late. If you are late, you are forgotten." Kelly lived by this motto. It was another piece of her training from athletics she carried with her into the real world. She instilled the same concept into her players.

Grace also followed this motto. On many occasions, Grace would often arrive at the gym before Coach Janssen. It was uncharacteristic for Grace to not show up early, so Kelly's concerns heightened as time ticked away and she was still not at the court. Kelly sent Grace texts, but no response. She tried calling, but still no response. Maybe Grace was just running a little late or traffic was heavy, Kelly wondered. She started warming up and shooting. Before she knew it, a half hour had passed. Grace was nowhere to be seen.

Kelly tried calling Grace again. The phone continuously rang before going to voicemail.

"Hey Grace, it's Coach. I just wanted to check in to make sure you were okay. I thought we were meeting at 10. It's 10:30 now, so I will stay until 11. Please call me when you get this."

Grace being late was one thing but not communicating and being a now show was completely out of character. Kelly's concern increased. She wrapped up her workout and headed home at 11:15 a.m. Kelly became so emotional she

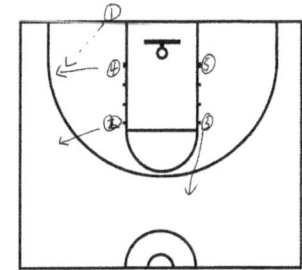

was fuming and frustrated. "Why do I even waste my time anymore?" Kelly said aloud in her car. She was disappointed and upset. She spent a great deal during the week preparing to share *The R.I.S.E. Playbook* with Grace. Her mind continued to wander to reasons why Grace did not show up.

Kelly dorve to the nearest coffee shop. She passed on her morning coffee to get to the court early. This was a mistake because she was extra grumpy. "I just don't understand. All I wanted to do is help, but I guess it is just never good enough," she said aloud.

"I'm sorry?" a voice rang out from the drive-thru speaker.

"Oh goodness!" Kelly responded. "I'm so sorry. I was thinking out loud, I guess. Yes, I would just like a regular black coffee. No, wait. Scratch that. I'll have a large Americano. I obviously need the caffeine."

As Kelly proceeded through the drive-thru, she realized she left her basketball at the outdoor court. She decided to go back to the court to see if it was still there. She calmed down from her fleeting moment of anger, pulled into the parking lot, and noticed someone was on the court shooting with her ball.

Kelly got out of her car and yelled, "Hey! That's my ball!" Rebounding the ball, the individual turned around. It was Grace.

"Grace? Where have you been?" Kelly asked.

"I'm so sorry, Coach," Grace responded. "I don't have any excuses. To be honest, I woke up this morning, and I didn't have any desire to get up. I'm sorry I didn't answer your texts or calls, and I'm sorry to make you worry. I just didn't have it in me to respond."

Kelly sighed. She was still upset, but she also appreciated Grace's honesty.

"Grace, are you okay?"

"Have you ever felt like you were drowning, Coach?" Grace asked. "Like no matter how much you try to keep your head above the water, you feel like there is someone beneath you who has a hold of your ankle and won't let go?"

"Funny you say that because I one-hundred percent know exactly what you mean," Kelly replied. Kelly could relate to this as it was similar to her drowning nightmares she had as a kid. It was the exact feeling she had this entire past year. She took in a deep breath and the two stood in silence for a few minutes.

"Coach, would you still have time to train me today?" Grace sheepishly asked.

"I can make time. Let's sit down first," Kelly replied.

There was a bench right next to the court where Kelly usually kept her bag or other items she brought from her car to the court. The two sat down and stared off into space for a few moments. Then, Grace broke the ice.

"So, what is our training lesson today?" Grace asked.

"The release," Kelly said.

"Huh? What do you mean? Like your shooting release?"

"Well, you can't stand on the court with the ball in your hands forever," Kelly said. "At some point, you have to release it. Like all of this pain and frustration we have built up. We have to release it and move on."

Grace nodded. "Yeah, I guess it is time for us to close that chapter, huh?"

"Yep. Then we need to forgive ourselves and forgive those who hurt us. We can't really move on until forgiveness happens."

Grace took a deep breath. "So, I have to forgive God?"

Kelly did not know what to say initially. She felt angry at God, too. To some extent, she blamed God for taking away her purpose in life. At least that's what her mind was tricking her to believe. She could understand why Grace would have such anger at God. She paused and looked at Grace. "I can't imagine everything you have gone through, Grace. But I can certainly understand why your anger would be directed at God. Have you told God how you feel?" Kelly said.

"Told God?" Grace replied sarcastically, flailing her arms into the air. "What? Like shouted into the sky, 'Hey God, I'm angry at you!' You can do that?"

Kelly smiled with a laugh, "Yes, that's exactly what I mean. I'm serious. To be honest, I've done my share of yelling at God recently.

He's a big God. He can take it."

"You are telling me you have really yelled into the sky and told God you are mad," Grace replied confused.

"Yep. Not long ago, actually. Seems kind of stupid, right?" Kelly said.

"Not stupid. I'm more afraid God would strike me down by a lightning bolt," Grace said. "Isn't it like not allowed or something to get mad and yell at God?"

Kelly smiled. "God created our wide range of emotions. So, I guess I've always assumed God understood when we express anger, even if it is at Him."

"I don't want to be this person to say this, Coach, but why are YOU mad at God?"

"What do you mean, Grace?" Kelly was confused about why she said this.

"I mean, you think God took away your coaching job, right? Is that why you are angry?"

Kelly looked at Grace with a look she often gave her on the court when Grace would say the exact thing Kelly was about to tell the team, but Grace would beat her to the punch.

"I know it probably seems like it, but I don't think God took coaching from you. People have their own agendas. Blame them, not God," Grace said.

Kelly was speechless. She sat back and gazed into the sky, trying to fight back emotions. Grace leaned over, clutching the basketball with her forearms resting on her knees. She looked at Kelly's face.

"Coach, did you ever think maybe your purpose is just getting redirected?" Grace asked.

Kelly again tried to choke back tears. She could not look at Grace because she knew she would start sobbing, and she hated crying in front of anyone.

Grace stood up and took a step onto the asphalt court. She walked to the middle of the court and stopped. She turned back towards Kelly.

"Coach, I know you grew up in church," Grace continued. "Did you grow up Catholic, too?"

"No, but I have been to about every church you can imagine, even Catholic," Kelly giggled. "Why do you ask?"

"I just don't understand how there are so many churches," Grace continued. "How do you pick the right one? How do you know they aren't all just a waste of time?"

"That's a great question, Grace. To be honest, my best answer for you is to share my own personal beliefs. I believe in having a personal relationship with Jesus. I think the key is you need to find a place of worship that aligns with the truth of Jesus and where you can grow in your relationship with Him. At least, that is what I look for."

Grace shook her head, not so much in agreement with Kelly, but because a flurry of thoughts began racing through her mind. She gazed at Kelly briefly before she turned around towards the court. Music was playing in the background. A song lyric rang out "Just let go-o-o-o-o-o." Grace took a deep breath and threw the basketball she had in her hands as hard as she could into the sky.

"GODDDDDDDD!!!!!!" she screamed. Grace sprinted to one end of the court and turned around and sprinted to the other end. The ball fell from the sky and bounced a few times before rolling towards Kelly, who was still watching from the bench. Grace continued to sprint back and forth the length of the court. With every stride, she wept harder and harder. Her face grimaced with each breath. She ran until her legs would no longer move. She made it near the middle of the court and again collapsed. Now on the ground, Grace, on her hands and knees continued to sob. Grace yelled, "God, I'm so angry! Please make the pain stop!"

Tears streamed down Kelly's face as she stood and walked to Grace. Kelly knelt and put her arm around Grace to comfort her. "He will, Grace. He didn't do this to you. He's here to hug you and help you through the pain. He loves you."

10
ELEVATE

The moonlight scattered beams of light onto the dock. The lake appeared to be glistening as the water currents gradually flowed. The sky was clear. The wind was motionless, yet there was a slight chill in the air.

Kelly found herself in the lake only about 10 feet from the dock. Submerged in the water from the neck down. The problem was she could not get herself to the dock because she felt paralyzed. Her limbs would only move enough to keep her head above the depths of the lake. Her chin would occasionally dip down and submerge, generating mouthfuls of water she continuously had to spit out. She did not know how much longer she could stay afloat.

Everything around her was still. She only heard a faint chirping of an orchestra of crickets and the water faintly splashing against the dock. She hoped someone would find her soon.

Suddenly, she felt a hand grab her ankle and yank her down below the surface. Her eyes shut. She could now only hear her heartbeat. As everything became dark, she again felt a hand grab her. But this time, the hand grabbed her forearm and began pulling her out of the water as quickly as she was yanked under. She opened her eyes and saw a blurry figure in radiating light above the water.

She felt the hand around her ankle release as her upper body was forcefully exiting the water. She heard a voice whisper, "rise," as she felt her body rapidly approaching the dock.

Just as Kelly had a clear vision of the figure, she felt a jolt springing her upright in her bed.

Her phone was ringing. Gasping for a breath, she answered the phone with a groggy, "Hello?"

"Rise and shine, KJ!" the voice echoed.

"WHAT?!" Now awake and realizing she must have been dreaming, Kelly tried to

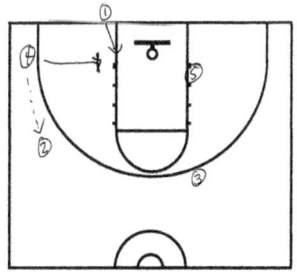

gather her bearings to form a sentence. "Who is this?"

"KJ, it's Peyton! Oh no, I woke you up! Are you okay?"

Still trying to catch her breath, Kelly replied, "Oh, Peyton. I'm okay. I just had a really weird dream. The phone startled me."

"I'm sorry, KJ. Well, hey, I'm calling you for your monthly wellness check. I know we haven't really had an opportunity to talk, but what do you think about your new playbook?"

"It's good, Peyton," Kelly responded. "Where in the world did you get this? It looks like it has been through hell and back."

Peyton laughed, "It's been very loved, but I can't take the credit. It was all God....well, written through Coach T. When she gave it to me, she made me promise to give it to someone who needed it more than me someday. I've been waiting for years, and it was so evident it was to go to you now. So, it's on you now to pass it on."

Coach T was Kelly and Peyton's high school basketball coach. She was also their first organized basketball coach when they began playing the summer prior to fifth grade. The high school hosted a youth camp and summer league annually, and Peyton and Kelly were selected to Coach T's team. She taught the girls basic fundamentals and basketball skills that Kelly and Peyton built their foundation of their entire basketball careers on. They reunited with her for the entirety of their high school careers. She was very tough, but they adored her. Kelly modeled a lot of her coaching style after Coach T.

"Okay...are you sure you are fine?" Peyton prodded. She could tell something was wrong by Kelly's voice.

"In all honesty Peyton, I'm just trying to keep my head above water and survive right now," Kelly said.

"Sometimes that is all you can do. Survive and Advance. And, that's okay," Peyton continued. "But here is the thing. It's time for you to stop living in the pain and start living. What I have learned is no matter how low and broken I feel, there is a warrior that lives inside me that will rise and put me back together into a stronger version of my old self. God gave each of us the warrior spirit that allows us to rise and overcome our brokenness and adversity that we face. This is what allows us to RISE."

Kelly let out a loud deep breath, "I know, but I'm afraid to fail... again."

"If you have that mentality, you can't rise, KJ. Most of the greatest successes stem from failing first. It's not about the miss. It's about the rebound. How many times have we witnessed in a game when a team puts up a three in the final seconds and misses it, it always seems to be on the kick out offensive rebound that a team hits a three pointer to tie or win a game. What if the player was too afraid to take the first shot or wasted too much time trying to find the perfect shot? It wouldn't have led to the opportunity for the attempt that was successful. It would be a greater tragedy if you didn't take the shot and at least try, KJ. And if you spend too much time dribbling around the court, you may run out of time to get a shot off. Look, we may never realize or know all of the lives we make an impact in daily, but God does. And as your friend, I'm going to tell you God needs you to stop doubting yourself when He placed a light within you that needs to be shared. Stop wasting your dribble. Other people need to see your light, Kelly. It's time to let God use it. Use your dribble to do something. If some people can't see your light, it's only because their own demons can't stand it."

Again, Kelly sighed. She thought about how lucky she was to have Peyton as a friend. It was not a coincidence Peyton was in her life. It was obviously divine inspiration Peyton always seemed to know when and what Kelly needed to hear from her.

"I think you need to read through your playbook again," Peyton said. "Actually, read the intro to me."

"Right now?" Kelly questioned.

"Yes, ma'am! Let's hear it!"

The playbook was on Kelly's nightstand, so she opened up the notebook to the intro page and read aloud to Peyton:

What does it mean to RISE? Rise is basically a player's ability to elevate, right? You can think of it like the ability to get vertical off the floor for a rebound, to block a shot, or to shoot a jump shot or layup, or even their ability to quickly get up off the floor after a fall. So, metaphorically speaking, how quickly can you rise after a fall or a loss? I really started thinking about this from a basketball team point of view. Basketball has taught us so many great life lessons, and what greater one than the ability to bounce back from a loss. Let's face it, life is hard. And our ability to overcome adversity is key. If we don't, we self-destruct.

We were made to be great, not to fall apart. Remember, we had to work on our plyometrics, our weight training, our conditioning, and our flexibility to become stronger to improve our verticals. The ability to rise is a process. We have to go through these things to become stronger, so we can help others rise, too. Training is not a one time endeavor. It's an everyday commitment.

Don't stay living in the pain. Satan would love nothing more than to keep you in your feelings, and for you to continue to live in doubt and fear. After a fall, it would be easy to just stay lying on the court. It can take a toll on you to try to get up, especially if you are injured, exhausted, or feel like it is too late to make an impact on the play now. But warriors are built to rise.

When you have to be the pillar of strength for someone else while navigating through your own adversity, it can become overwhelming. Coach T created The R.I.S.E. Playbook as a strategy to guide others to rise after a fall and to continue to help those in our care do the same. As Coach always instilled in us, these lessons are well beyond just the court. So, I hope this acronym helps you as you RISE from your fall, Kelly.

"But first, you have to let go and get up, Kelly," Peyton reiterated. "This is a process not an overnight fix. Let go, get up and forgive. Not just those who you thought wronged you, but you need to forgive yourself. It's time to live again."

Kelly sat silent on the phone. For the first time in over a year, she finally fully understood what "getting up" meant. It wasn't going through the motions like she had been for so long. Like Peyton said, it wasn't just surviving, it was living.

"Do you remember when I cost us making it to the championship game," Peyton asked Kelly.

"Peyton, you did not lose us the semi-final game. You gave us a chance to win." Kelly refuted.

"Well, I felt like I lost that game then. I missed, and I took a shot I shouldn't have taken. You were wide open. It was a poor decision, but a great learning lesson. I was so down after the game. I don't think I ever told you this. I was off by myself crying, and Coach found me. And that's when I was introduced to *The R.I.S.E. Playbook*. It really helped me and continues to do so. Now let it help you."

"First off, Peyton. You know I am not as good of a shooter as you. So how do you even know we still wouldn't have lost?" Kelly asked.

"Because I believe in you," Peyton responded. "I've always believed in you. You are my lifelong teammate, and I know how special of a player and person you are...back then and now."

Kelly sheepishly grinned, "I don't understand why..."

"Why what?!" Peyton interrupted. "I believe in you? Stop it, and let me help you."

"How do you always seem to know when I need you to give me a swift kick in the butt?" Kelly asked.

"Let's call it divine intervention," Peyton responded. "I'll let you go live now, but keep me posted. And you know, the phone works both ways. I'm here whenever you need me."

"I know, Peyton," Kelly replied.

"I know you are struggling with your purpose. I was just thinking about the other day when we were in the playoffs and saw the Psalm 20:4-5 scripture. Do you remember that?" Peyton asked."

"May he give you the desires of your heart and make all your plans succeed. May we shout for joy over your victory and lift up our banners in the name of our God. May the Lord grant all of your requests," Kelly recited. "I remember that scripture fondly. It was one of the few I memorized and can actually remember. We thought God was telling us we were going to win the championship and raise a banner in the gym. I guess we misunderstood that scripture at 17-years-old, didn't we?"

"Yes, we did. God's not a genie, and we can't just pick and choose scriptures that fit our agenda and make us feel good, you know? The Bible is God's living word. It's active and alive. It's crucial to study the context of the scriptures of the verses, the history of the time it was written, and most importantly seek God in it all," Peyton explained. "As a teen, I believed that Psalm meant God was going to grant us all our wishes, desires, and plans. I now understand the context of what King David wrote. Simply put, God has a plan and purpose for our life. Our hearts can be deceptive. When we chase after our own heart's desires without placing God at the center, we're not truly pursuing HIS purpose for our lives. True success comes when those desires are aligned with God's will. This doesn't always mean we'll achieve exactly what we want, but we will fulfill what He has designed for us. God created us to long for Him, but the fall in the Garden of Eden disrupted our connection, causing us to question our identity and drift from the truth that we belong to our one true Heavenly Father."

"Goodness. I had no idea you turned into this biblical philosopher, Pey," Kelly teased.

"Who knew, right?!" Peyton joked back. "Hey, I surprise myself sometimes. Or maybe God just puts the words in my mouth He wants you to hear. That seems more realistic, honestly."

"Thanks, Peyton," Kelly said grinning ear to ear. "I hope you know how much I appreciate you."

"I do. Don't go getting sappy on me. Just go get those TOTS, my friend," Peyton said.

Kelly ended the phone call. She looked down at the playbook. Her eyes were glued to the question, What does it mean to RISE?

The acronym, R.I.S.E., a concept to overcome adversity in basketball and in life, seemed like a simple four step process. But as Peyton said on the phone and Kelly had finally realized, it was going to be a process that was going to take time. It was not meant to be an instant gratification, self-improvement, 20-minute video to help you feel good in the moment.

Her mind shifted to the nightmare Peyton awoke her from by calling. It was a long time since she had those nightmares of drowning in the lake. This dream felt different. She tried to remember what the voice whispered.

"Wait...it said rise!" Kelly exclaimed. "Was that just coincidence or something else?"

R.I.S.E.

R: REDISCOVER YOUR WHY.

I: IGNITE YOUR PASSION.

S: STRENGTHEN YOUR SUPPORT SYSTEM.

E: EMPOWER OTHERS.

This concept, as Peyton explained, was to help you fully rise after a fall. The first step is getting up, but then you have to rediscover your why, ignite the passion within you, strengthen your support system by utilizing those who care about you, and empower others to rise.

Kelly knew this was the perfect training lesson for Grace.

She hoped by sharing these concepts with her, they would rise above everything they both had gone through in their lives. Together, it was time to rediscover their identity and pursue their why. Kelly did not know exactly where God may be directing Grace, but she knew she had a purpose to play a part in the journey to Grace's why.

As she went on with her day, running errands, doing laundry, and prepping for her Sunday meeting with Grace, Kelly's dream flooded her thoughts. After she made herself dinner, she sat down and started binge watching her favorite television drama. One episode she began watching was a flashback to a scene which reminded Kelly of the emotional pain Grace exhibited the prior week. The scene featured one of the main characters flashing back to the moment her grandfather died, feeling helpless as she watched her mom have a panic attack as the realization of his death overcame her. The scene was too familiar to Kelly's own experience the day Grace had the breakdown on the basketball court. Kelly needed to get all of these things out of her system, so she pulled out a piece of computer paper and began sketching.

As Kelly began sketching, she recalled a picture of Grace shooting a layup which she had hung in her coaching office. Shortly before she was fired, she gave the photograph to Grace, as she was updating her office decor. Kelly was inspired by this photograph, sketching the basketball player she had committed to memory. She sketched a hand coming out of the court, grabbing the player's ankle to symbolize her feelings of her poem line, "hardwood heaven full of sin." Kelly sketched lines to make the court appear as though it was made of water. It represented both Kelly's dream, but also how she felt sometimes with life. She looked at basketball as a gift from heaven trying to save her, but something kept pulling her away from God.

Kelly was pleased with her sketch. Given she had not sketched in 15-20 years, it looked better than she ever anticipated. She folded it up and placed it in a pocket in the back of the playbook.

At last, Kelly felt a sense of accomplishment from her productivity. She wound down for the night with a shower and bedtime preparations. Tomorrow was going to be the start of an epic comeback, she thought. She was inspired and ready to conquer the training lesson with Grace. She rolled over in her bed, turned off her nightstand lamp, and drifted off to sleep.

11

REDISCOVER

A powerful sensation of déjà vu infiltrated Kelly's body. She saw herself once again treading water in the middle of the lake, feeling a mixture of panic and eerie stillness from the familiarity of the situation. Suddenly, she was dragged beneath the surface and then lifted back up just as she was about to take her last breath. This time, however, she was pulled onto the dock, gasping for air as she tried to cough the water from her lungs. Looking ahead, she saw the figure who rescued her walking towards a misty, white fog beyond the shoreline. Just as the figure was about to vanish into the mist, it stopped and slightly turned around. As the figure looked towards Kelly, she woke up.

Kelly sat straight up in her bed. Breathing heavily, she wondered why she was having these dreams again. It had been years since she had these nightmares, and more than ever before, she had questions. Who was this figure? What do these dreams represent? Is she dying in the dreams and going to heaven? As a child, her dreams were incredibly vivid, and they felt even more realistic now. However, the dreams she had the past two nights were a bit different than what she remembered from her youth. She didn't remember a figure pulling her out of the water but only a hand. She usually woke up as she was submerged under water.

Catching her breath, Kelly glanced at her nightstand and saw the playbook Peyton had given her. Though she had no memory of bringing it to bed, she hoped reading Peyton's words might soothe her morning anxiety. She grabbed the playbook and began reading.

She began with "R" in R.I.S.E. to the page entitled Rediscover.

R: Rediscover your why.

Dreams and goals are important to set and pursue, but the reality

is we don't always achieve them. We live in a society that glorifies rewards, accomplishments, participation trophies, and instant gratification—but that's not how the real world works. Life isn't always fair. You can do everything right, work harder than anyone else, show up consistently, and still not get the promotion. The truth is, despite our best efforts, things sometimes don't go our way.

From a basketball offense perspective, it's annoying to see a junk defense thrown at you. As you know, the goal of a junk defense is a disruption that creates confusion and frustration that will lead to turnovers and defensive stops. I like to think of life in this way when we face adversity. Sometimes, life throws you junk defenses, disrupting your plans, your dreams, and your goals. If you don't have a strong foundation of fundamentals, it is easy to get flustered and let the junk defense dictate what you do on the court. Like junk defenses, it's easy to let adversity in life dictate your attitude and how you move forward if you don't have a strong base of fundamentals and a resilient mindset.

Just because you face junk defenses doesn't mean you just willingly turnover the ball and stop fighting to win. First, you need to rely on your training to identify the junk defense. This means being calm in the midst of chaos and being mentally tough and staying positive. The best way to handle pressure is to be aggressive and attack it. By doing this, you will eventually find the holes in the defense. Learn to be comfortable being uncomfortable.

Coach T's basketball philosophy was to win the key three stats — turnovers, free throw percentage, and rebounds. More often than not, if you win those three stats, you will put yourself in a position to win the basketball game. These stats are the stats teams have the most control over. Like turnovers, free throw percentage, and rebounds, if you control the controllables in life, such as attitude, mindset, and your effort, you give yourself a chance to win.

The next step in rediscovering your why is forgiveness. Forgiveness is complicated. It is also necessary to fully move on in this process. As difficult as it may be, let go and let God deal with those who wronged you. I know you, KJ, and I know you are still experiencing a lot of inner turmoil. I don't think you realize how much blame you put on yourself. Don't forget to forgive yourself.

How many losses did we experience as a team because we weren't playing our game? We let the other team dictate how we played. We lost because we lost our identity and we forgot our why. After experiencing a loss, you have to rediscover what makes your team special by going back to the basics.

Life is a lot like this. When we have a major loss or fall, we tend to lose our identity. Sometimes it's easy to let others dictate our view of ourselves. Negative actions or comments against you may make you start to question who you are and whether you are good enough. Your identity is the first thing attacked. And if we forget our identity, we forget why we play. We forget what makes us tick. We forget about our why and what got us there in the first place. You have to rediscover your identity to rediscover your WHY. The first step to RISE is to Rediscover who YOU are and WHOSE you are. Jesus never said we wouldn't go through storms. But, remember who walked on water. The defeat doesn't define you. Let God use it to refine you.

Finally, remember your basketball training. God blessed us with this incredible gift of basketball. Use it for His glory. So, to rediscover your identity in Him:

1. Lose with grace.
　　　　·Come to Jesus with a humble heart.
　　　　·Take accountability.
　　　　·Don't play the blame game.
　　　　·Forgive others, and forgive yourself.

2. Watch game film and review the stats.
　　　　·Take a self inventory on where you might be missing the mark.
　　　　·Rediscover your identity. Where are you in your relationships? With God?

3. Study your playbook and communicate with your coach.
　　　　·Open those lines of communication.
　　　　·Talk to your mentor(s).
　　　　·Focus on your WHY.

This will help you rediscover who you are in Jesus and rediscover your why.

　　　Kelly read the playbook previously, but for some reason this time reading the Rediscover section resonated with her differently than before. She acknowledged she felt like she lost her identity in all of this, especially in her relationship with Jesus. Perhaps the dream symbolized moving on to the next chapter, she mused. Life mirrors the mystery of what is hidden in the mist. She felt peace looking into the fog, and she felt like she was constantly drowning by just going through the motions like she was now.

As she continued thinking about the idea of rediscovering her identity and her why, Kelly looked at the clock and realized it was time to get ready to go to the outdoor basketball court. She was meeting Grace to begin their training session, and she now had the exact lesson they were going to discuss.

Grace was early to the basketball court, already getting up shots when Kelly arrived. Kelly was happy to see Grace there, back to her normal self and in good spirits.

"Hey, Grace," Kelly said as she walked onto the court. "It's good to see you."

"You, too, Coach," Grace replied. "So, what's today's training consist of?"

"Well, we are going to talk about *The R.I.S.E. Playbook*," Kelly responded.

"Ooh, *The R.I.S.E. Playbook*. I like that," Grace nodded. "So, you have a playbook to teach us to rise up?!"

Kelly chuckled, "Yes, basically. A really great friend of mine taught me this strategy. I know I need it, and I thought we could take this journey together. I thought we could work on one concept each week."

"Sounds good to me, Coach," Grace smiled.

"R.I.S.E. is an acronym. Today, we are starting with the 'R,' which is REDISCOVER," Kelly explained. "Rediscover means rediscovering your identity and your why."

"On the basketball court?" Grace asked.

"Not exactly," Kelly laughed. "In life."

"Okay, so who I am, and what is my purpose?" Grace asked. "Wow, so it's like that, Coach? We are going deep?"

"Yup," Kelly replied.

"Yikes, Coach. You've got me thinking this deep early in the morning?" Grace said as she put up another jumper. "Is this kind of like a punishment for me being so late last time?"

Kelly laughed, "No, this is for you and me to heal and grow."

Grace continued shooting. "Alright, well I'm ready to rise then. Let's goooooooo!"

Kelly smiled and grabbed *The R.I.S.E. Playbook*. She began reading the Rediscover section to Grace. She tried to relate the stories of Peyton and Kelly's team to when Grace played. They shared stories about their high school teams. They reminisced about the good times, the incredible plays, and the team bonding when Grace played for Kelly. They laughed a lot, but the mood turned somber. It was evident they both realized their wounds had not healed and left permanent scars. The memories led them to recognize the absence of a team environment, and how much they missed being a part of a team.

"You know, Coach," Grace said. "This hits close to home. I think I forgot what makes me feel alive. I know I've not had it easy in life, but I've always had basketball—in the good times and the bad times. It was the bond I shared with Trey and Nana. It keeps me close to them. I wouldn't be here if it wasn't for basketball."

Grace paused, dropped her head, and looked down at her shoes. Kelly could tell she was trying to choke back tears and collect her thoughts. Kelly knew this past year particularly was difficult for Grace. She did not want to upset her, but she also sensed Grace needed to move on.

Grace continued. "When you got fired, it was about the same time I suspected something was seriously wrong with Nana. Basketball wasn't the same. I felt like I wasn't wanted anymore. It felt like I was being blamed for everything going wrong with the team. Then Nana got really sick, and I just quit caring about basketball anymore. I quit caring about being a part of a team. I've just felt so lost. Even shooting now, I don't know. I just feel...empty and alone."

"Basketball has always been an important part of my life, too,"

Kelly said. "You are not alone. I'm always here for you. I know how you feel because I have felt the same. You know, when I got fired, I felt like a piece of me died. I stopped caring about everything. I felt so empty inside. The day I first saw you on the court, it was only recently I picked up a basketball."

Kelly took in a deep breath, "But then I went home, and I remembered why basketball was an important part of my life. It was because God gave it to me as an outlet. I've also just realized He gave it to me to use as a tool."

"What do you mean by a tool?" Grace asked.

"A tool to use to make a positive impact on others," Kelly replied. "I love basketball. I always have. Sure, I'll be the first to admit sometimes it becomes more of an obsession or an idol than it should be. God wouldn't have given me this desire if there wasn't a purpose behind it. I could use basketball as a platform to help younger people grow and find their purpose in life. Then, it hit me...that's MY why. Since I didn't have a person who lifted me up when I needed it in college, I want to be that for someone else."

Grace smiled. "I truly believe you have made an impact on so many people. You aren't afraid to show us how much you care. And I, for one, really needed someone who cared. You'll never really know how much I needed that."

Kelly grabbed the ball out of the net after Grace again nailed a deep three-pointer. Kelly was always in awe of how Grace appeared as if she was barely trying when she had a ball in her hands. She was an incredibly gifted player, which made Kelly heartbroken, thinking about Grace's outlook for her final year.

"Thank you, Grace. I know basketball has been a sensitive subject, but are you going to play this next season?" Kelly asked.

"I can't," Grace sighed. "I just can't. It's not what it was for me. I'm afraid if I try to play it's going to make me completely hate the game, and I don't want that."

"I understand. It's weird how similar our stories really are." Kelly replied. "Look, for us to rediscover our why, I think we both need to completely let go of everything that happened to us. Sure, we need to remember the past to rediscover our identity, but then we need to move forward. Please, go forward, don't totally shut the door yet on next year."

"Okay, Coach," Grace said. She ran to grab her rebound herself. She stopped in front of Kelly, and Kelly grabbed the ball from her.

"What's your why, Grace?" Kelly asked.

Grace looked Kelly directly in her eyes, almost as if she was gazing into her soul, but then she looked down at her own feet. Grace realized no one had ever asked her this question before. She thought for a minute, raised her head, looked Kelly again in the eyes, and smiled. Grace simply stated, "The same as yours."

12

IGNITE

Kelly arrived home after the workout with Grace. Grace was in high spirits as they left the court, which warmed Kelly's heart. She felt like she was making a difference again. After running some late errands, she walked into her house and proceeded to her walk-in shower. Her mind suddenly shifted to racing thoughts about how she should have approached coaching differently. She turned on the water and stood under the showerhead for what felt like hours, letting the warm water penetrate her pores. As the water hit her face, her mind transported back to the life changing rainy Good Friday. She replayed conversations and moments in her mind all over again. She was emotional standing in the shower, thinking about what she could have done better. This happened frequently. Daytime joy gave way to evening doubt and regret.

She got out of the shower and got ready for bed. She bumped her nightstand while walking by and heard something fall to the floor. As she bent over to pick up the object, she realized it was *The R.I.S.E. Playbook*. She felt an urge to journal the moment her fingers touched the leather. She sat down and started jotting down notes on the back pages of the playbook.

As she continued writing notes, she thought about the characteristics of what makes a great team. Perhaps she was overlooking these elements when she coached. As a coach, having talent and a brilliant game plan for a team is important, yet the most important piece of assembling a team is building leaders. Kelly believed she did everything she could to help her players develop their character and leadership. Amid the pressure to recruit, win games and balance her other role at the university—she lost sight of focusing on team growth. Her why was the players. Her why was loving them and using basketball to foster their growth in their integrity, discipline,

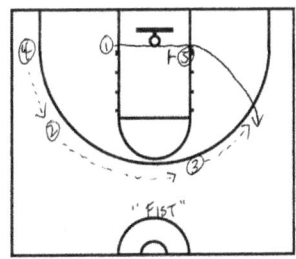

discipleship, emotional intelligence, self-awareness, and resilience. Most of the players she encountered were broken. She was once in their shoes as a college player, and she valued the opportunity to guide them to wholeness. Ultimately, she wanted to lead them to the hope she found in her relationship with Jesus. But as the pressure mounted, she neglected the why.

That night, Kelly once again dreamed she was in the lake. Like the previous nights, she was treading water, pulled beneath the surface, then pulled out of the water and onto the dock. The figure who pulled her out of the water walked to the shoreline to the misty fog. But as the figure began to turn to look at Kelly, it stopped midway and turned its head slightly to the left, as though something caught its attention. Kelly was curious about what the figure was now looking at. As she hesitantly turned her head to the left, out of the misty fog suddenly appeared a sun beam which radiated light onto a basketball court. It was the glorious outdoor basketball court Kelly played on as a kid and what appeared to be another figure putting up shots.

Suddenly, Kelly felt this overwhelming rush of warmth flow through her body. She glanced down at her arms and saw what looked like a fiery, molten lava moving beneath her skin and throughout her veins. The vision was like any superhero movie Kelly had watched as a youth. She could only compare the feeling to the adrenaline she would feel before playing a basketball game. As she continued to feel the fire flowing down her body, she looked down at her fingers and then her toes–now glowing. When she looked back up toward the mist, she woke up.

As she opened her eyes, she was confused and unclear of where she was. Regaining her senses, she realized she was in her bed and not upon the dock. The word passion was ringing repeatedly in her mind. Perhaps this is the reason a basketball court appeared in her dream. To Kelly, it made sense the lava flowing through her veins symbolized her passion. She remembered the second principle of RISE—ignite. She grabbed the playbook and began rereading what Peyton wrote.

I: Ignite your passion.

Remember when we were juniors? We lost one game all
season. We had these hopes and dreams to make the
final four, but we lost in the regionals of playoffs.
In the blink of an eye, those dreams were shattered.
We could have hung our heads and gone into the next
year with doubts about our team, but we didn't. We
hated how we felt after that loss, and we never wanted
to experience that feeling ever again. Our passion
ignited because we desired to achieve our dream.
We worked hard, invested in a common goal, and we
accomplished it.

Once you rediscover your why, you have to find the
spark within you to set those goals and dreams.
Then, the fire of passion will ignite to pursue and
accomplish YOUR why. When your passion ignites,
there's no telling what you can accomplish because you
are going to focus, push through the wind, work, and
run the race of your life because you are going to
remember what it felt like when you lost your spark.
Be grateful for this game, the wins, and the losses
because look at all you have learned that has helped
you in life. Always practice gratitude.

But what happens when you experience the dreaded
shooting slump? We've all experienced it. Shooting
slumps are frustrating. They are incredibly difficult
to work through. As a shooter, your first instinct is
to reevaluate your form. You try to correct it, which
sometimes can lead to overcorrecting. Overcorrecting
can become a mental block. Focusing too much on
"fixing" your shot can lead to more harm than good.

This is why it is important to go back to the basics, trust your muscle memory, and refocus your mindset. The power of the mind is fascinating. It can be our sanctuary or our battlefield. Mental conditioning is vital as an athlete, and it is vital in life. Like basketball, training your mind takes practice and time. It's not a one day, 30-minute training. It is an everyday grind. Remember what Paul taught us in Romans 12:2, "Do not conform to the pattern of this world, but be transformed by the renewing of your mind. Then you will be able to test and approve what God's will is—his good, pleasing, and perfect will." (NIV) God gave us a blueprint for mental conditioning.

Once you go back to the basics, concentrate on your training routines to keep your mind focused and present. Refocus your mindset to go out and play like you did when you first started playing basketball. You played because you LOVED the game. Play free—no pressure, no stress, no worries. Think back to when you were a little girl, when those hopes and dreams and your passion for basketball first began. Search for THAT joy. God gave you a unique gift. He gave you those hopes and dreams for a reason. He has a plan for you. Feed your mind with nothing but positivity.

When we were having a really off shooting game or just not playing our best basketball, Coach T always said there are other ways you can contribute. And it never fails—when you focus on the little things that don't show up in the stat sheet—the rest of the game comes to you. Focus on mastering the fundamentals and I guarantee you will find the burning fire within you again. Ignite your passion, and you'll find your purpose.

Be alert because there will be doubters and haters that will spew negativity towards you. And if you don't properly condition your mind, those negative thoughts and self doubt will also creep in. Where do you think those thoughts of self doubt, unworthiness, and lies come from? They don't come from God. Just like God uses people for your good, Satan will use people to tell you that you can't do something, you aren't good enough, you can't accomplish your dreams, or that God doesn't care about you. Silence the haters. It's not what they think but what God can do.

Ignite your Passion:

1. Go back to the basics.
   - Focus on the fundamentals.
   - Find ways to relax and recharge.
   - Don't continue to live in a season of pain.

2. Do the little things that don't show up on the stat sheet.
   - Build healthy habits.
   - Control the controllables.
   - Acts of kindness are healing.
   - Practice gratitude.

3. Search for your joy in the game.
   - Do the things that give you joy.
   - Feed your mind with positivity.
   - Silence the haters.

Kelly always viewed her passion as basketball. Lately, this spark of passion was very dim. She lost all confidence in her knowledge and reasons behind why she wanted to be a basketball coach. One person's view changed her heart, and she did not understand why this weighed so heavily on her.

She grabbed her phone and dialed Peyton's number.

"Hello?" Peyton answered.

"Hey Peyton, it's Kelly." Kelly anxiously replied. She needed Peyton's wisdom.

"Hey KJ, what's going on? Are you okay?" Peyton said with concern.

Kelly continues. "Yeah...I've just been having these weird dreams lately. And well...I don't know. I don't know if they have to do with this entire experience or your playbook or—"

Peyton cuts off Kelly mid-sentence. "Woah there, KJ. Take a breath."

Kelly felt a bit defeated. "Sorry. So, I've been having these odd dreams, and last night there was a basketball court and this human figure shooting. I don't know what it means, but maybe it's because I've been having these really great workouts with the player I told you about when I was home. Long story short, but I ran into her at the court I was working out at. We started having these "training" sessions. I'm actually meeting her soon. Man, this kid is going through it, and I'm trying to help her. She's doing a little bit better, but I just cannot get rid of this sinking feeling I'm just going to fail her again."

"KJ, I'm going to stop you right there!" Peyton interrupted.

Kelly looked up at the ceiling. Her eyes began to well. She knew what was coming. She had a sinking feeling in the pit of her stomach.

"You know I love you, and I have to say this to you as a friend. Please know this is completely out of love. I told you the comeback process would be painful." Peyton continued. "KJ, you don't have the ability to save people. Only God does."

"But Peyton, I'm not trying—" Kelly tried explaining her point of view.

"Not trying to save her? Oh, but you are. I know you. You care so much for other people, and where you think you are finding your joy is 'helping and saving others.' But dude, you are literally killing yourself because you think you have to do this alone and fix everything. You think it's an expectation others have of you that you are going to come save the day. You are also putting God in a box. You've got to drop your cape, and give it to God. Yes, I firmly believe God has placed you in the lives of others to plant seeds. But girl, let Him cook. Stop trying to do His job."

Fighting back her emotions, Kelly bit her tongue and responded, "I know."

Peyton could sense Kelly was trying to push back tears.

"Kelly Janssen. There is absolutely NOTHING you can do to change what happened. But you can change how you fail forward. Yes, I said fail forward, meaning you can't let the fear of failure keep you from moving forward. If you fail, so what?! At least you tried. At least you learned something from it. And God will redeem it. Mark my words. But the crazy thing is you didn't fail this kid and you won't because God has a purpose for you and for her. God's not going to waste your pain. We may fail as humans, but He won't. He isn't going to fail either of you. Let God do His thing. Get out of the way. Let go and move on. Stop letting an experience of failure define you. Let it refine you. You've held onto this pain and fear too long. You either have to play through it or quit. And the Kelly Janssen I know is no quitter. So, stop sulking and get better." Peyton lectured.

Kelly sighed, "okay."

"Okay!" Peyton exclaimed. "Let me hear it! I didn't believe your soft 'okay."

"OKAY!" Kelly screamed.

"That's what I'm talking about! Now, go to the court. Do your thing. Be positive. Let God cook. Fail Forward."

Their conversation ended, and Kelly readied herself for the day, gathering her gear for her basketball session with Grace. She held back from really speaking her mind to Peyton because she was honestly too

115

mentally exhausted to get into an argument. Deep down, she knew what Peyton was saying, but she did not want to accept it. Kelly's mind was a battlefield, and she did not know how to explain to someone else the mental, emotional, and spiritual battle she was experiencing.

As she climbed into her car, she thought perhaps speaking with Grace about the "I" of RISE would shed light on igniting her passion and getting her out of her own funk. Maybe finding purpose again would get her mind out of turmoil.

When Kelly arrived at the court, Grace was already in full-on workout mode. She was running sprints into full court layups.

A bit winded, Grace exclaimed, "Hey, Coach!"

"Hey, Grace," Kelly said in a somber tone.

"What's wrong?" Grace asked.

"Nothing, I've just been having these weird dreams, and I guess I'm just not quite getting the rest I need." Kelly explained.

"Do you want to talk about it?" Grace asked.

"No, I'm good, but thank you." Kelly finished stretching and walked over to Grace. "It's time to be in the present. Are you ready to get started?"

"Did you not just see me sprinting, Coach?" Grace laughed. "I already started.. Let's goooo!"

Kelly giggled. It was the first time in a long time Grace's infectious personality was shining. It was refreshing. "Ignite. That's the next lesson."

"Ignite? Like are we going to light a fire or something, Coach? I'm not sure how I feel about burnt offerings. Weirds me out a bit." Grace laughed.

"Sort of. Just kidding, Grace," Kelly smirked. "But yes, you are going to sort of light a fire within you. You are igniting your passion."

"Oh, I get it. But isn't that what we are already doing?" Grace asked. "Getting back on the court and getting a ball in our hands. We love basketball. Isn't that how you ignite your passion? You immerse yourself in it."

"Well, well, well. You are pretty wise, Grace Villanueva," Kelly sarcastically responded as she snatched the basketball from Grace's hands.

Grace grabbed the basketball back and winked at Kelly. "Yeah, I know."

116

13

SUPPORT

Kelly's parents, Axel and Anne, moved to the East Coast before Kelly's career eventually led her to the same city. Although Axel and Anne shared many common interests, their personalities couldn't have been more different—yet they balanced each other beautifully. Anne was a charismatic, outgoing, natural social butterfly, until health issues began to dim her light. A talented singer and artist, she spent several years teaching English at a Christian-based school. Axel, on the other hand, was quiet, steady, and dryly witty. An engineer by trade, he also had a hands—on creative side and took joy in building and fixing things. He rarely showed strong emotions—unless a spider crossed his path. He was the anchor of the family, a constant source of strength and calm, and his love for Anne and their daughter, Kelly, was unmistakable in the way he navigated their emotional highs and lows with patience and grace.

After years of therapy, Anne's mental health vastly improved. She developed significant physical health issues when Kelly was in college. As Kelly matured, it troubled her to be living so far away from her aging parents. The opportunity to move closer to them was the most ideal situation for the family. Axel and Anne were incredibly supportive and missed watching Kelly and her teammates play, so they were thrilled when Kelly relocated to the area to pursue her coaching career. Axel and Anne, self-proclaimed super fans, followed the team for hundreds of miles to support both the players and their daughter. They also hosted dinners for the team. Anne loved cooking her famous fried chicken for all the girls. Grace particularly connected with Anne, giving her the nickname "Mama Sweet Pea" after Anne slipped and called Kelly "Sweet Pea" during one of the meals in front of the team.

Nearly every Saturday and Sunday, Kelly would visit her parents' house in the early afternoon for a late lunch and

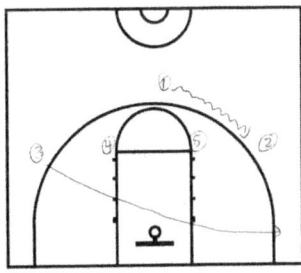

family sports time. They were three peas in a pod, a close-knit, sports fanatic, Jesus-loving family.

When Kelly's coaching dream fizzled, her parents tried to lift her spirits by reminding her God had a plan. After one football-filled Saturday, her mom recalled an event from many years ago.

"Sweetie, do you remember when you bought me the rocking horse for Christmas?" Anne asked.

Christmas Memory — The Rocking Horse

While in college, Kelly worked part time at a home décor store. One day, while unpacking a new shipment, she came across an item she knew would be the perfect gift for her mom. Her mother adored rocking horses, loved Christmas, and was a gifted singer and guitar player. This rocking horse was a larger figurine featuring Santa sitting atop the horse, with a base designed to resemble a music staff with notes—a beautiful blend of her mother's passions.

As a struggling college student, Kelly diligently saved up her money to afford the special gift. Just before heading home for semester break, she proudly purchased the rocking horse, eager to surprise her mom.

On Christmas Day, Kelly was thrilled to give her mom her gift. When Anne opened it, she cried with joy; she loved it. As the day went on, the family prepared their Christmas meal, and the rocking horse sat proudly on an end table. While Kelly was turning a corner to fetch something from the living room for her mother, she accidentally brushed against the horse, sending it tumbling to the ground. It shattered into several pieces, leaving Kelly devastated.

"What happened?! Are you okay?" Anne asked.

"I broke your horse," Kelly said as tears flowed down her face. "Mom, I'm so sorry. I ruined it. I ruined the most perfect gift I ever got for you. I've ruined Christmas."

"Oh, Kelly," her mom said calmly. "You didn't ruin anything! It's just a thing. You are my most precious gift."

Kelly sat on the floor crying. She was distraught by the incident.

A few moments later, Axel came out of the basement after working on some projects in his tool shop.

"What happened?" he asked.

"We had a little accident." Anne replied.

"I broke mom's rocking horse," Kelly said as she was trying to pick up the pieces of the horse figurine.

"Kelly, you go help your mom with dinner. Let me clean this up. I've got it," Axel replied.

Anne helped Kelly up off of the floor. They walked to the kitchen to prepare Christmas dinner. This helped Kelly get her mind off of the accident. Her father picked up the pieces of the broken rocking horse and swiftly took them down to his shop in the basement. About an hour later, her father emerged from the basement.

"Kelly!" Axel hollered. "Come in here for a second."

Kelly and Anne came into the living room from the kitchen.

"You fixed it?!" Kelly exclaimed. She could not believe her eyes.

Axel had meticulously glued the figurine back together, making it look as if nothing had happened. He mounted it on a stained wooden base, which provided the once top-heavy figurine with added support, balance, and stability. The repairs were barely noticeable unless you looked closely.

"I got lucky," Axel whispered to Anne. "I found the stained board downstairs and it was a perfect fit."

"It wasn't luck," Anne whispered back. "It was God."

Back to present day

"There is a great lesson in this, Kelly," Anne said. "Sometimes we fall, and we break. But just like your father did Christmas morning so many years ago, your Heavenly Father will also pick you up, glue you back together, and make you stronger than you were before you fell. You may still be able to see the scars, but those scars remind you of what you overcame."

Kelly often recalled this story with fondness. Her parents' unwavering faith in God inspired her, yet she continued to struggle with her own feelings of anger and doubt. Despite her efforts to help Grace move on and to heal herself, she still felt a disconnect in her relationship with Jesus. She persisted with her daily devotionals, attempting to relate them to her training sessions with Grace. It was evident Grace was seeking a relationship with Jesus, but Kelly found it challenging to find the right words to discuss God with her and adequately answer her questions.

The Saturday before, Kelly was to meet Grace for a training session on the next lesson from *The R.I.S.E. Playbook*, she went to her parents' home for their Saturday sports day. As Kelly walked in the house, her dad was already in his favorite Lazy-Boy recliner watching a game. But her mother was not present.

"Where's mom?" Kelly inquired.

"Well, you know she didn't sleep again last night," her father replied.

"Again?"

"Yep, and she got sick in the night, too," Axel reiterated.

"And let me guess," Kelly annoyingly responded. "She didn't go to the hospital and won't call the doctor."

"Bingo," Axel said.

"Why does she do this?" Kelly asked her dad.

"I don't know, Chief," Axel said. He had called her Chief since she was a little kid. A term of endearment and representation of one of their favorite sports teams. He leaned forward in his chair and let out a frustrated sigh. "She's stubborn. That's why."

As Kelly took a seat, her mom came out of the bedroom, still in her pajamas, and seeming a little incoherent.

"Speak of the devil," Kelly chuckled. "Hi, Mama. How are you?"

"Not great," Anne responded.

Anne sat down on the couch and took her daily medication. She told Kelly she had vomited and had an incident falling in the living room the night before. Kelly was irritated with her mother for not taking a trip to the hospital when it was clearly needed.

"Mom, maybe you should go to the hospital or at least call the doctor on Monday," Kelly stated.

"I'm fine. This is just my normal, my broken body is just doing its typical weird things."

As the afternoon progressed and the family continued to watch the game, Kelly noticed her mom was starting to doze off. Anne was sitting up on the couch. She had a water bottle she had just taken a drink from. As she went to lower the water bottle, it appeared as she was so tired she began falling asleep as her arm drooped down. She was about to spill her water all over when Kelly ran over and grabbed the bottle.

"Mom, why don't you go to bed or lay down? You can't keep your eyes open." Anne had always experienced some version of sleep deprivation, even at an early age. But, over the past several months, it seemed to be worse. It was driving Kelly and her dad crazy.

"Mom!" Kelly exclaimed again. "Just go to bed already." She was annoyed because her mother would shrug her off and continuously spill drinks, food, whatever she was holding all over herself, the couch, and on the floor.

"Stop yelling! I'm not a baby!" Anne yelled angrily back.

"I just don't understand why you don't listen to anyone," Kelly said somewhat under her breath so her mother wouldn't completely hear what she said. She didn't want to start an argument with her. They were both incredibly stubborn and, ever since Kelly was a teenager, they both knew exactly which nerves to push.

The Janssens continued watching their game. Kelly would glare from time to time over at her father, then at her mother. They were both fed up with Anne's unwillingness to talk to the doctor about what had been happening.

After several minutes, Anne appeared to have passed out. Kelly looked at her dad. "Is she okay?"

"You know how she gets," her dad responded.

"Dad, I don't think she is okay." Kelly walked over to her mom and tapped her on the shoulder.

"Mom..."

Anne barely opened her eyes enough for Kelly to see them roll into the back of her head.

"MOM!" Kelly yelled.

There was no response. Initially, Axel and Kelly thought Anne was experiencing low blood sugar. Kelly ran to the kitchen and grabbed a juice while Axel found Anne's glucose tablets. They had experienced a similar situation before, so they assumed it was her diabetes. But as they tried to give her both the juice and glucose, she wasn't responding at all.

"Dad, call 9-1-1. This isn't good," Kelly yelled.

Kelly panicked and froze. Through coaching, she was trained in CPR/First Aid and other sports medicine related training. But this was different, and she felt completely helpless.

As the paramedics arrived, they determined quickly, it was not her blood sugar. It seemed to be her heart. The paramedics could find a pulse and help Anne gain consciousness, but they quickly loaded her on a stretcher and rushed her away into the ambulance.

Axel and Kelly stood silent in the house, almost as if they were frozen and did not know what to do.

"Kelly, grab what you need. Let's get to the hospital," Axel said calmly.

The car ride to the hospital was only about 10 minutes, but it seemed like two hours.

"Dad, she's going to be okay, right?" Kelly asked her father.

"I don't know, Chief," Axel responded. "Just keep praying."

Axel and Kelly arrived at the hospital and checked in at registration for information on Anne. There were no updates, so they took a seat in the waiting room. Unfortunately, this was not an unfamiliar place. Kelly spent countless hours as a child with her dad in hospital waiting rooms. They both seemed to go into a robotic mode, grabbing the nearest magazine and just finding ways to pass the time.

Time seemed to move slower and slower. Kelly was getting very antsy, and she told her dad she was going to find a vending machine. She walked over to the vending area and stared at the machine.

Something about gazing into the machine triggered the memory of the day in middle school when her mom overdosed on prescription pills. She flashed back to her dad, screaming at her to get in the car when she returned home from the basketball court. She stood in front of the vending machine in the hospital of her hometown, trying to choke back tears as she worried about her mom. Those memories continued to flood her mind.

Spacing off, she suddenly felt a tap on her shoulder. When she turned around, however, there was no one there. Confused by what just happened, she purchased snacks for her and her dad. She turned around to go back to the waiting room. As she took a step, she felt the presence of a being. She stopped and looked around. No one was near her.

"Did you find something," Axel asked.

"What?" Kelly asked. Her mind was still wandering off to another realm.

"In the vending machine? Did you find a snack?" Axel asked.

"Oh," Kelly sighed while handing Axel his candy bar. "Just a candy bar. Dad, you didn't come and tap me on the shoulder at the vending machines, did you?"

"No," her dad responded. "Why?"

"It's nothing," Kelly sighed. "I just spaced off for a minute and thought maybe someone was near me."

Kelly opened the wrapper of her candy bar and began eating. The presence of something supernatural was still close. She closed her eyes and took in a deep breath in between bites. She felt an overwhelming sense of peace flood her body. Her dad could tell she wasn't mentally present, but he didn't know what to say and went back to reading the waiting room magazine.

What seemed like hours had passed when a doctor finally approached the Janssens in the waiting room.

"Are you Anne Janssen's family?" the doctor asked.

"We are," Axel responded. "Is she okay?"

"She suffered a cardiac event, but she is stable. We are going to keep her for observation for a few days. We inserted a temporary pacemaker, so her heart is steady. She is sedated right now, so it would probably be best for you to go home and get some rest. We will contact you when she is ready to receive visitors."

Axel and Kelly simultaneously let out a sigh of relief. They knew the routine. They had been through this process more times than they could count. As much as they wanted to stay, they knew it was best to go home and try to rest. It would do no good for either of them to get sick from the stress of the day and the worry they had about Anne.

Neither Axel nor Kelly got much rest that night. Kelly got up in the middle of the night and started binging a television show. She found herself watching a show she and her mom would watch often together. For those few hours, she distracted her mind from what had happened and soon fell asleep on the couch.

The next morning, she awoke to a text from Grace.

coachhhh, where u at?

Amid the chaos with her mother, Kelly had forgotten to text Grace to let her know what was going on.

Kelly: Grace, I'm so sorry. Something happened with my mom. I can't make it. I'm so sorry.

Grace: oh no! coach, i'm sorry. i hope she is OK. u need anything?

Kelly: Thanks, Grace, but no.

Grace: OK coach. tell mama sweet pea her grace is sending lots of positive vibes and prayers her way.

Kelly: Thank you, Grace. I will. We'll talk soon.

The next few days became a blur. As Anne recovered and found out some of her medication caused this incident, Axel contemplated moving him and Anne back to Missouri. He always dreamed of retiring at the Lake of the Ozarks. After Anne's latest health scare, he did not want to waste time.

A couple of days after Anne was released from the hospital, Axel told Kelly they needed to have a family meeting. Kelly knew her dad's feelings about returning to Missouri. He had discussed retiring with Kelly previously. She knew in the pit of her stomach what he was going to say.

"Chief, we decided we are going to move back to Missouri," Axel said. "I know you came out here because we were here. Well, and basketball. But given everything you have gone through the last year, I really think you need to consider what you want to do."

"What do you think I should do, Dad?" Kelly asked. Being a daddy's girl, she often sought out his wisdom.

"Kelly, you know."

"But Dad, I can't just leave the university..."

"Why not?" Axel paused and looked deep into Kelly's eyes. "You have been miserable the past year. And the way they have treated you, you owe that place nothing. I think it is time to move on. And maybe we are the push you need. I really don't know why this is a question for you."

Kelly sighed. She knew he was right, but she hated change. And a piece of her deep down kept hoping she would magically go back to coaching like nothing happened. But reality was sinking in for her.

A few days later, Kelly received another text from Grace.

Grace: Coach, i hope mama sweet pea is healing. u okay?

Kelly: Yeah, but we need to talk in person.

Grace: Ok. do u wanna meet later today?

```
Kelly: Could we meet tonight at the court?

Grace: Works for me!

Kelly: Okay, is 8:30 too late?

Grace: No ma'am. 8:30 works for me, Coach. They got
lights! ;)

Kelly: Okay, see you then.
```

That Saturday afternoon, Kelly paced back and forth in her apartment. She decided to drive around for an hour before going to the court. Her mind was racing. As she had with countless drives before, she used the time to talk to God and lose herself in deep reflection. She arrived at the court early. She got out of her car with the playbook and walked around. She knew she had to tell Grace she could not train her any longer. There was too much going on in her life to make it possible. She thought Grace would understand, but she also knew she might be a little upset. The sun was beginning to go down when Grace pulled up to the court.

"Hey coach!" Grace exclaimed. She was dressed ready to workout. She thought when Kelly texted, they were going to chat and then continue with their workouts. Grace being Grace started firing off questions as soon as she saw Kelly. "How is your mom? Is she doing better? So, what's on the agenda today? Are we getting to the "S" of RISE?"

"My mom is okay," Kelly said somberly. "Well, she will be."

"Coach, I'm so sorry you have been dealing with this," Grace said as she walked over and gave Kelly a hug.

Choking back tears, Kelly squeezed Grace tightly. "Thanks, Grace."

Kelly pulled away abruptly, as she was embarrassed to ever let anyone see her emotional. "That's enough of that. Let's get to it. Yeah, the "S" is support."

Grace could feel Kelly's tension and reluctancy. "So, I guess our hug was unintentionally a great segue to support, huh?" she joked.

"I guess so," Kelly said with little reaction. "But let's just do some warmups and shooting drills for now. We can talk later."

"Okay, Coach," Grace said as she grabbed her basketball out of her bag. She sensed Coach Janssen wasn't in the mood to talk or even joke around – her demeanor was similar to how she acted after a loss or when the team slacked off during drills. Grace understood she just needed to give her space and let her focus on basketball for now.

After about 30 minutes of shooting, Grace finally broke the silence as she released a shot.

"So, are we going to talk about support or shelf the lesson for another day?"

Kelly grabbed the ball out of the net. She took a couple of steps toward Grace, stopped for a minute, took in a deep breath, and hesitantly said, "I'm so sorry, Grace, but I just can't train you anymore."

"What?! Why?!" Grace questioned. "We don't have to do the lesson today, Coach. We can talk another day. Stopping seems extreme!"

"I just can't. There's just a lot going on with my mom and with my life. I can't put in the effort you need from me."

"Coach, I understand you are dealing with a lot with your mom and with everything that happened this past year, but didn't you say basketball church could be like our place to heal...together? It seems like you are just running away because things are hard."

"That's not fair. You're just a kid and don't get it," Kelly snapped, more harshly than she intended. "I can't help you right now!"

"So it's like that, huh? In other words, you can't be there for me like you promised?" Grace replied, noticeably upset by Kelly's response. "Figures. No, Coach. You don't get it!"

"Grace, I'm sorry. Please try to understand I just can't do this right now. You don't need me anyway," Kelly took a step closer to Grace and handed her the playbook. "Here."

Reluctantly, Grace took the playbook and responded.

"Understand what, Coach? You promised to always support me. What an ironic joke! I should have known better. You put on this facade like you are here to help everyone, but you are just like all the others, like the AD, like all those girls. You are just in it for yourself. No wonder we had such a toxic culture. You just abandoned us. But, I'm just a 'kid' so what do I know?!"

"Hold on! That's uncalled for!" Kelly yelled back.

"Is it?! You say you believe in me, but I know what you really think. You even said you didn't think I would make it in life. You just think you can 'save' all these broken, misfit toys because you are like God's gift or something. It's always about you. You are too selfish and arrogant to see our team failed because of YOUR pride. You don't get to decide what I need and what I don't. Take your stupid playbook back. I don't want any of this!"

Grace threw the playbook at Kelly and stormed off.

"Grace, what are you talking about?! I never said you wouldn't make it in life. What would ever make you think I would say that?! You know me better than that!" Kelly was so thrown off by Grace's reaction she ran after her, grabbed her arm, and pulled Grace back towards her. "Grace, we need to talk! I know you are disappointed, but where are these comments coming from?!"

"LET GO OF ME! LEAVE ME ALONE! YOU ARE NOT MY COACH! YOU'RE NOBODY'S COACH! I DIDN'T NEED MY PARENTS! I DIDN'T NEED TREY! I DIDN'T NEED NANA! AND, I CERTAINLY DON'T NEED YOU!" Grace screamed.

Grace emphatically pulled herself away from Kelly's grasp and dashed to her car. She locked her car doors and sped off with her tires squealing.

Tears streamed down Kelly's face as she struggled to comprehend what had just happened. Grace's sudden outburst left her bewildered, the impact of it hitting her like a ton of bricks. Overwhelmed by her emotions, she squatted down, tears streaming as panic took hold of her breathing.

Her chest tightened, hands trembling, and a high-pitched

ringing filled her ears. Everything around her seemed to fade into silence, as if the world had been muted, leaving only the rapid drumming of her heart beat and her quick, shallow breaths. She felt as if she were drowning in a full-blown panic attack, unable to find a way to the surface. As she opened her eyes, she realized the playbook was still in her hand. It was opened to the "S" of RISE:

S: Strengthen your support system.

There's no "I" in "Team." We weren't successful on the court all those years because of one player. We were successful because we were a great team. We each had strengths in different areas. We made sacrifices and were willing to serve each other. We accepted our roles for the ultimate goal. We only succeeded by working together and moving as one. It's easy for people to love your team in the good times. But in the bad times, the support you get sometimes only comes from each other. We were successful because we had a strong foundation and a strong support system.

In team sports, it takes everyone to be successful, especially defensively. We shifted on the court as one single unit. Not everyone loves playing defense like you do, nor were we all as good as you were at it. You were a great example of a player who denied her own selfish ambitions for the good of the team. Our team played terrific help defense, and you were a big reason why. I knew if I got beat off the dribble or on a backdoor cut, you were ALWAYS right there to assist and shut down my man. You had a knack for knowing exactly where to be at exactly the right time. My confidence came from the trust and confidence I had in you. Don't forget in life when you feel defeated, you

131

should have confidence your teammate is behind you to pick you up, especially Jesus. He knows exactly where to meet you at exactly the right time.

The most successful people in the world did not gain success by pursuing it alone. They have a circle of support. We aren't supposed to carry the burdens of life by ourselves — God did not create us to be solo. That is why Jesus is our support and provides us with those who can help us on our life path. Surround yourself with people who hold you accountable, uplift you, encourage you, and are good for your soul. Let others help you rise and help others rise, as well.

To strengthen your support system, there are a few things you have to do. Focus on becoming a great teammate. How can you help your teammates in life? Communicate with your teammates and work on ways to bond as a "team." Work on building those relationships again and find opportunities to fellowship with your support system. Make the relationships God has placed in your life a priority. Be present for your teammates. Listen to understand and practice empathy. Strengthen your support system to succeed.

Strengthen Your Support System:

1. This is a team sport.
        •You are not alone.
        •We need each other to win.
        •surround yourself with people who uplift you and are good for your soul.

2. Communicate on the court.

- Keep an open line of communication with your teammates.
- Share your feelings and what you are experiencing with a teammate.

3. Become a great teammate.
   - Make your relationships with your teammates a priority.
   - Team bonding is important.
   - Be present.
   - Listen to understand.
   - Put yourself in your teammate's shoes.

Consumed with despair, Kelly screamed and hurled the playbook with all her might. She walked over to the bench near the court and sat down to work on some deep breathing exercises to calm herself down. With tears streaming down her face, she sat in silence staring into the night sky, trying to slow her breaths for what seemed like an eternity.

The anxiety and adrenaline finally subsided. Kelly wiped the tears from her eyes, took her car keys out of her pocket, and went to sit in her car. She waited for a couple of hours, hoping Grace would return to the court. As midnight approached, Kelly felt a numbness engulf her. Exhausted, she realized Grace was not returning, and it was time to head home to sleep away the mental unrest.

14

TURNOVER

The heat waves of summer faded into a distant memory. The fall semester was well underway, and Kelly was in the height of college recruitment season — the whirlwind of campus tours and events, college fairs, and recruitment visits to high schools. She buried herself in her work after her parents moved back to Missouri in October. The days blurred together in a routine of long hours, draining drives, and quiet dinners alone. When the air turned crisp and the leaves changed colors to radiant hues of red, orange, and gold, Kelly was too caught up in her monotonous schedule to notice nor did she care.

As autumn turned the page to winter, the leaves fell, and the temperatures dropped. The turnover of seasons was in full swing and so was basketball season. Every time Kelly strolled through the hallway and caught sight of her former team's new poster, memories flooded back to her. The poster featured the new season's team and schedule. Many familiar faces of Kelly's past players and former recruits, but there were also a lot of unfamiliar faces. She noticed one face was glaringly missing...Grace.

Kelly had not heard from Grace in months. She was uncertain whether Grace was still enrolled in classes or even attending college. She never saw her on campus, although she remained isolated from former players. A rumor circulated the athletic director had ordered them not to be in contact with their ex-coach following her dismissal. Despite her partial understanding of the reasons, it still caused her pain. She did not want to create any type of drama or distraction, so she continued to stay distant. They were moving on with their life. She needed to move on with hers.

Concerned for Grace, she couldn't shake the thought Grace had distanced herself for a purpose. Perhaps Grace's words about Kelly

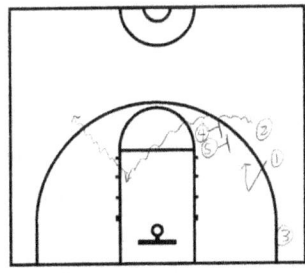

held some truth after all. After more than a year of self-reflection, she realized she had forgotten the source that granted her the platform of basketball. She felt ashamed to admit pride had taken hold, and she hadn't placed God at the forefront of the team.

Throughout the academic year, Kelly existed in a state of emotional detachment. Instead of seeking friendships, she withdrew from social interactions and ceased all discussions related to basketball and the events of the past year. She no longer concerned herself with others' opinions. Instead, she focused on her recruiter work. Her life had fallen into a routine of work, followed by returning home.

As the dead of winter trudged on, Kelly started applying for coaching and athletic positions in Kansas and Missouri to be closer to her parents. Following Peyton's advice, she embraced the notion of failing forward. She contacted other coaching connections to find viable opportunities that may open up but nothing sustainable transpired. She was discouraged.

Kelly continued looking for months to no avail until one spring day she received an unexpected text from a former college classmate who suggested a position that was open at Kelly's dream university growing up. She fantasized playing basketball at this Division 1 powerhouse, but she knew she was not mentally or physically equipped to play at this level during this period of her life. The opportunity to work for this school was appealing. It was not a coaching position or even a position in athletics, but it was an opportunity to go to her birth state of Kansas.

Life in her current position was quite chaotic. There was a turnover in recent years in her office, which led to her boss adding more and more responsibilities to Kelly's plate. Exhaustion set in and she experienced burn out. The joy she once had for student recruitment was gone, especially since coaching was no longer a factor.

Kelly grew up in sports, learning many transferable skills, such as time management, how to work with a team, having a high work ethic, being organized, practicing discipline by following rules, and staying on task. She was efficient with her work, but she knew her lack of care was affecting her performance, and she hated this. She found it ironic she was commended for her quality of work. In fact, she found it disheartening because, for many years, she had toiled tirelessly with minimal recognition. Now, she felt her efforts were lackluster, yet she was receiving more praise than ever before.

Maybe it was time for a change. She pondered the opportunity for a few days and then began an application for this potential new job. She was not even sure it was a good fit, but as her father encouraged her, it was a foot in the door.

As the spring semester was drawing to a conclusion, Kelly was tasked with assisting as a proofreader for the graduation program. She scanned through the program, cross checking spellings of graduating seniors' names. Her heart pounded as she scanned the list of the business majors and approached the V last names:

Derek Taylor
Jessica Thomas
Kevin Tran
Allen Vallor
Ashley Vanmeter
Grace Villanueva

Kelly smiled. She was so relieved to see Grace's name on the graduation program. She let out an enormous sigh, slow and weighted, because she knew she would not see Grace walk across the stage. Kelly could not attend the graduation ceremony. She was offered the job she applied for back home several weeks ago. She put in her notice. Over the weekend, she traveled to find housing before permanently moving. Although Kelly could not attend graduation, she wanted to make sure Grace knew she was thinking about her. She hoped maybe someday Grace would forgive her.

She found a graduation card, inserted a little bit of money, and penned a heartfelt letter to Grace.

DEAR GRACE,

I KNOW YOU ARE PROBABLY STILL UPSET WITH ME. I'M
SO SORRY I FAILED YOU. UNFORTUNATELY, I WON'T BE AT
GRADUATION TO SEE YOU GET YOUR DIPLOMA, BUT I WANTED
YOU TO KNOW I WAS THINKING ABOUT YOU. I AM SO
INCREDIBLY PROUD OF YOU. I WISH WE COULD HAVE TALKED
ALL OF THIS OUT, BUT I ALSO UNDERSTAND WHY YOU WANTED
NOTHING TO DO WITH ME. I NEVER SAID YOU WOULDN'T
AMOUNT TO ANYTHING IN LIFE. I HAVE NO IDEA WHERE YOU
HEARD THAT OR WHY YOU WOULD EVER THINK I WOULD
SAY THAT ABOUT YOU. HONESTLY, IT BREAKS MY HEART YOU
WOULD BELIEVE THAT LIE. I BELIEVE QUITE THE OPPOSITE
ABOUT YOU, AND I HOPE YOU WILL CONTINUE READING TO
UNDERSTAND WHY I THINK YOU ARE SO SPECIAL AND WHY I
BELIEVE GOD HAS AN IMPORTANT PURPOSE FOR YOU IN THIS
LIFE.

I'LL BE HONEST, THIS IS NOT AT ALL WHAT I ENVISIONED YOUR
GRADUATION WOULD BE LIKE. WHEN YOU STARTED COLLEGE,
YOU WERE THIS BRIGHT-EYED FRESHMAN WITH THE ENTIRE
BASKETBALL WORLD AT HER FINGERTIPS. YOUR ENERGY
AND EXCITEMENT FOR NOT ONLY BASKETBALL, BUT LIFE WAS
INFECTIOUS. AND WHEN YOU HAD A BALL IN YOUR HANDS,
YOUR INFECTIOUS ENERGY AND PASSION TOOK EVERYTHING
TO ANOTHER LEVEL. I REMEMBER I WOULD JUST SIT BACK
AND WATCH YOU ORCHESTRATE YOUR GIFT ON THE COURT,
AND I THOUGHT "THIS KID HAS IT." YOU HAD THE "IT" - THE
THING YOU CAN'T TEACH. I LOVED WATCHING YOU PLAY. IT
WAS POETRY IN MOTION. I'VE BEEN FORTUNATE TO HAVE

CHEMISTRY WITH A TEAMMATE BEFORE - THE UNSPOKEN "CONNECTION" THAT IS HARD TO DESCRIBE BUT YOU FEEL IT IMMEDIATELY. YOU KNOW WHAT THE OTHER PERSON IS GOING TO DO BEFORE THEY DO IT. YOU DON'T HAVE TO SAY A WORD. IT WAS A BLESSING TO ALSO EXPERIENCE THIS CHEMISTRY ON A PLAYER/COACH LEVEL WITH YOU.

IN MY MIND, YOU WERE THE KEY TO THE CULTURE SHIFT. WHEN I SAW YOU INTERACT WITH YOUR TEAMMATES, I KNEW WE WERE ON THE RIGHT TRACK. YOU WERE GOING TO BE A BIG REASON WHY. YOU WANTED TO BE GREAT. YOU UNDERSTOOD WHAT EXCELLENCE LOOKED LIKE, AND YOU WANTED TO BE THE ONE TO HOLD YOUR TEAMMATES TO A HIGHER STANDARD. I WOULD JUST SIT BACK AND WATCH YOU LEAD. I ENVISIONED CONFERENCE CHAMPIONSHIPS, PLAYOFF RUNS, AND CONFERENCE AND ALL-AMERICAN HONORS SPECIFICALLY FOR YOU. I THOUGHT WHEN WE ARRIVED ON THIS DAY, I WOULD BE WATCHING YOU WALK ACROSS THE STAGE AS ONE OF THE MOST DECORATED AND SUCCESSFUL PLAYERS IN OUR PROGRAM'S HISTORY.

BUT I GUESS SOMETIMES GOD SAYS, "NO."

I MAY NEVER UNDERSTAND WHY GOD SAID NO. I'VE ALWAYS KNOWN YOU HAVE A GREATER PURPOSE THAT EXTENDS WELL BEYOND WHAT BASKETBALL COULD PROVIDE YOU, BUT THIS ISN'T AT ALL WHAT I IMAGINED WOULD TRANSPIRE OVER THE PAST TWO YEARS. AND I DON'T KNOW, I LIKE TO HOPE ONE DAY WE WILL LOOK BACK ON THIS EXPERIENCE AND REALIZE THE ONLY WAY TO REALLY ACCOMPLISH OUR PURPOSES

INVOLVED WALKING THROUGH AND SURVIVING THESE STORMS. GOD HAS A BIGGER PLAN FOR YOU, AND I HAVE TO BELIEVE ALL OF THIS HAS MADE YOU SO MUCH STRONGER AND SET YOU UP FOR ONE EPIC COMEBACK. YOU ARE GOING TO IMPACT AND CHANGE LIVES. I HAVE NO DOUBT ABOUT THAT.

JUST AFTER I WAS FIRED, YOU LEFT ME A NOTE ON MY DESK THAT READ, "HAVE A GOOD DAY! #3 :)" I STILL HAVE THAT NOTE. YOU ALSO SENT ME A TEXT I SAVED THAT SAID, "WE ALL HAVE ROUGH TIMES. JUST KNOW YOU ARE NOT ALONE. LOVE YOU COACH!" THOSE MAY HAVE SEEMED LIKE LITTLE THINGS, BUT TO ME IT WAS SOMETHING I DESPERATELY NEEDED AT THAT MOMENT. YOU WILL NEVER KNOW HOW THOSE LITTLE GESTURES KEPT ME GOING IN A VERY DARK TIME IN MY LIFE. THANK YOU FOR YOUR LOYALTY AND ALWAYS HAVING MY BACK. MY ADVICE TO YOU IS TO KEEP THOSE LITTLE POSITIVE NOTES YOU RECEIVE (I CALL THEM TOUCHSTONES) BECAUSE, TRUST ME, ONE DAY YOU WILL HAVE A HORRIBLE DAY AND NEED THOSE REMINDERS TO REMEMBER YOUR WHY AND TO KEEP YOU GOING.

SPEAKING OF, I DECIDED IT WAS TIME FOR ME TO MOVE ON AND GO BACK HOME. I HAVE ACCEPTED A NEW POSITION IN KANSAS, AND I WILL BE MOVING THERE SOON. IF YOU ARE EVER IN THE MIDWEST, PLEASE REACH OUT. I HOPE ONE DAY WE CAN SPEAK AGAIN.

I DON'T KNOW WHERE YOUR JOURNEY WILL TAKE YOU, GRACE, BUT GOD'S GOT YOU AND HE LOVES YOU, KIDDO.

REMEMBER, YOUR NAME LITERALLY MEANS "FAVOR IN GOD'S EYES." THERE'S A PLAN. THERE'S ALWAYS A PLAN. IT MAY NOT BE WHAT WE PLANNED, BUT HE'S GOT A PLAN FOR YOUR GOOD. DON'T FORGET WHO YOU ARE AND WHOSE YOU ARE. YOU'LL ALWAYS BE MY #3.

CONGRATULATIONS! *Love ya, kiddo.*

GOD BLESS,
COACH JANSSEN

Kelly mailed the card to the last address she had for Grace. She prayed it was still where she was living, and she hoped she would at least read it. After dropping off the card at the post office, she called Peyton.

"Hello?"

"Hey Peyton, it's KJ."

"KJ! It's been a while, friend! Hey, a little birdy told me you were moving back this way?!"

Kelly giggled, "that little birdy was correct. I got a new job. It's still as a recruiter, but a little different. So, I don't know. We'll see how it goes."

"Well, I'm happy to hear you are coming home. We will definitely have to get together. Actually, there are some reunions coming up this summer, so I'll keep you in the loop about those."

"Okay, sounds good," Kelly responded.

"So how are you? I know we haven't caught up in some time. But how are things going besides lots of changes?"

"Yeah, I know, and I'm sorry for not keeping you in the loop. It's just been a crazy year. Although that's not a great excuse. It's just been a lot, and I guess I was just keeping to myself and trying to figure stuff out."

"I get it, KJ. But remember, you have support! Hey, how did the training go with that kid you were telling me about. Did she play this last year? What happened?"

"Well," Kelly's voice changed to a more somber tone as she paused for a second. "Unfortunately, I don't know what happened to her, except I know she graduated."

"Oh," Peyton replied somberly. "I'm sorry to hear that."

"It's okay," Kelly said. "I mean, it's not okay, but it is what it is. Things were going really well, and then some stuff happened with my mom. Mom's okay now. I mean, as okay as she is going to be. And I had to walk away from the training, and well, it went over like a lead balloon. Grace just pretty much cut me out of her life. I haven't heard from her since last summer."

"I'm sorry that happened, KJ," Peyton said. "But she's young. And, I think I said this to you before, but you can't save everyone. Only God can. Maybe you were just sent into her life for a season, you know. If not, you'll see her again. Don't lose hope."

"Yeah, I guess so," Kelly replied. "I actually just dropped a graduation card in the mail for her, which I'm hoping she at least reads. And as much as my heart hurts, I know I just have to let her go at this point."

"You do. And remember, you have other students that need you to plant the seeds."

The two continued on with their conversation before Peyton had to take one of her children to a practice.

"Let me know when you are officially moved," Peyton said. "You'll be back home soon. Love you, KJ!"

15

LOVE & BASKETBALL

Kelly's personal relationships suffered for years. Outside of her job, she found it difficult to meet people. For many years, she was married to basketball, her dedication undivided, solely focused on the game. When she was fired, her coaching mentor, the men's basketball coach for Lions Park, advised her to treat the loss of her coaching job as a divorce. She grieved it. She missed basketball deeply, still harboring love for the game despite the pain it caused. When she refocused her attention on God and as time passed, things began to change, particularly her heart.

Her transition to this next chapter of life was an adjustment, but she was overall pleased she moved back to the Midwest five years ago. She never realized how much she really overextended herself all those years. Kelly enjoyed her new colleagues and the slower pace of everything. She also formed a close bond with a small group of fun, supportive women who quickly became her crew for Target runs, dinners, girls weekends, and much needed laughter. Although she continued her recruitment career in a different capacity and developed new friendships, she still felt like something was missing in her life – someone to share it with.

Kelly's standards for love were almost unattainable. Friends and family believed she was holding out for the unrealistic expectation of a Hallmark movie. Her standard was set by the example she witnessed between her parents. Axel's love for Anne embodied the kind of marriage God intended—reflecting the unconditional love Jesus has for us. Her dad was the standard by which Kelly measured every man she met. She trusted God's timing and was at peace with waiting for the man He had chosen for her—and even with the possibility such a man might never come. She found contentment in singleness. But after losing basketball and realizing the space it took up

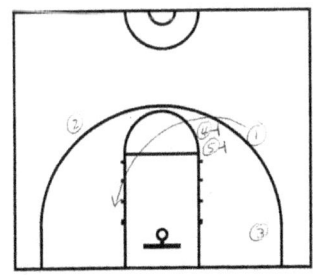

in her heart, a quiet tug stirred a deeper longing to find this kind of love.

March was one of Kelly's favorite months. She often referred to basketball's March Madness as second Christmas. Every year, she would take the first weekend of the month off to watch non stop basketball. Watching the first full weekend of the NCAA Division I Men's and Women's Basketball Tournaments was something she enjoyed annually. The electric energy, the unexpected upsets, the nail-biting finishes—it was the kind of thrill she usually lived for. But this year felt different. There was a quiet anticipation in the air, a stillness tugged at her, though she couldn't quite explain why. This holiday felt less important. The adrenaline and joy she felt watching games was not present. It was just another weekend of basketball. Nothing special.

She realized she needed to grab dinner and was craving sushi. There was a local bistro downtown which was only a few blocks from her apartment. She often ordered carry out there. Tonight, she decided to dine in. Kelly walked a few blocks downtown to the bistro. She walked in and took a seat at the bar, ordered a beer and sushi, and began watching the basketball games on the televisions behind the bar.

She paid for her meal and was finishing her beer when a gentleman brushed her back, walked behind her and sat down directly next to her at the bar. She paid little attention to him until he tapped on her arm.

"Sorry to bother you, ma'am, but is this your silverware?" he asked.

"Oh, I'm so sorry. I apparently tend to spread out when I'm eating," Kelly said as she grabbed the silverware and moved them to her empty plate.

"No worries." He smiled and reached out his hand to shake hers. "Hi, I'm Jaylen."

"I'm Kelly. Nice to meet you."

She returned his handshake and found herself gazing into his eyes. Tall, light-eyed, and dark-complexioned, he was exactly her type. He possessed a million-dollar smile, and his eyes were truly

148

captivating. She saw his kindness, yet also something mysterious.

In her recruitment travels, it was not uncommon for Kelly to strike up a conversation with strangers in restaurants, but this interaction caught Kelly off guard. This was certainly not an interaction she expected as she was finishing her meal.

"Have you been here before?" Jaylen asked.

"Yes, I come here all the time. I guess I'm kind of a regular. I love sushi. I live and work close by, so it is really convenient."

"Excellent. What sushi do you usually get, or what would you recommend?" Jaylen asked.

"I love the poke bowl and really anything with ahi tuna," Kelly replied. She felt somewhat distracted by his eyes and falling into a trance like state. She didn't want to seem creepy, but he was just so intriguing and attractive.

"So, how about you? Have you been here before?" she asked.

Jaylen smiled. "Yeah, you could say that."

"Okay?" Kelly half-laughed. She tended to laugh when she was feeling uncomfortable.

Jaylen grinned looking down at his menu, "I wasn't planning to come in to eat, but I guess life works weirdly sometimes. So how is your bracket looking?" He turned to Kelly and grinned, then winked at her.

She melted. She wondered: Was he flirting with her? She was so wrapped up in coaching basketball and her players, there was little room for other relationships. It had been a long time since feeling a spark with someone. Her heart fluttered, similar to how a preteen felt when a crush acknowledged her. It was a bit of foreign territory for her, so she tried to play it cool and just appreciate the opportunity of meeting someone new.

Kelly responded to his question about her bracket. "Oh, yeah it's probably going to end up like a dumpster fire, like it does every year. How's your bracket?"

"Surprisingly, it's doing pretty good so far," Jaylen smiled back at her. "It's usually busted by this point, so I'm hopeful this is my year!"

Kelly felt a sense of comfort and connection with Jaylen. He was easy to talk to and soon found herself chatting away about March Madness. Kelly rarely felt an instant soul connection with someone, only a handful of times. He seemed interested in her, asking questions about her life. She mentioned to him she had played college basketball and coached.

"I'm sorry to be forward, but why aren't you coaching basketball anymore?" Jaylen asked. "The way you talk about it seems like you really love it."

Kelly clammed up and hesitated. "It's...a long story."

"I've got time," Jaylen said, leaning in and listening closely.

She looked directly at him, then looked up. "It's hard for me to talk about it. I guess even after all these years it still is painful. Basically, I thought I had found my purpose in life. I felt like God had given me this great gift to coach and use the game I love so much to mold these young women, and I feel like I just screwed it up. I got fired a few years ago from a coaching position."

Kelly looked up at the ceiling and took in a deep breath. She was trying to choke down the tears and emotions attempting to surface. She just met this guy. He seemed awesome, and she did not want to scare him off by unloading her emotional drama on him. She was worried if she was too vulnerable, he would find her unstable and broken.

"Sounds like there is a lot more to this story," Jaylen interjected. "I played college basketball. I understand the politics of it all. The coach who recruited me and I played for most of my college career was fired before my senior year, so I get it. I'm happy to listen." He leaned over and gently placed his hand on hers. He looked deeply into her eyes and continued, "seriously. I'm a really good listener."

He seemed so genuine and kind. Kelly shared her background with basketball. She told him about her experiences playing and how she fell into coaching. She shared how she felt like God had provided basketball when she needed an outlet to cope with the heavy burdens of life.

"May I be frank with you?" Jaylen asked.

150

"Yeah sure." Kelly reluctantly responded. She wasn't sure what he was about to say, and she was nervous she shared too much.

Jaylen continued, "I know I don't know you, but from an objective perspective, it seems like you may have wrapped up your identity in basketball. And you are obviously struggling to find yourself again without it. Who said you had to be without it? God restores, you know."

The concept didn't fully register until a stranger voiced it. Kelly was completely overcome with emotion and started crying. She couldn't contain her tears. Turning to Jaylen, she locked eyes with him as tears streamed down her face. He reached out, placing a comforting hand on her shoulder.

"I'm sorry, I don't know why I'm so emotional right now," Kelly said.

"I think the holy spirit is working on your heart. If your identity is defined by the idol and the idol is taken away, you will fall apart," Jaylen reiterated. "Just like a house that does not have a firm foundation when a severe storm hits, it will be ripped apart and destroyed. This is why it is so important to make sure your foundation is strong because when, not if, a storm hits, you may have some scars and need to rebuild, but the foundation will still be there."

Kelly wiped her tears from her cheeks. She was enlightened by his comments. "It never clicked until you just said that. This gift God gave me, my own little Garden of Eden or what I like to call my Hardwood Heaven, Satan made me question my identity in Jesus and look for it in the wrong places. I found myself instead of running to Jesus in those heavy moments running to basketball. Instead of using this gift God blessed me with to draw closer to Him, I was making it my idol. Instead of finding my identity in Jesus, I was finding my identity in this sport. Wow. It sure has taken me a long time to realize my hardwood heaven was full of thorns."

"Look, I know how you feel," Jaylen continued. "I've done the same thing. I did it with my career. I got lost, and it took me a long time to find my way back to God again. God never said he wouldn't allow you to go through the storms. But what He did say was he would be with you through them."

Wow. This guy seems legit, Kelly thought to herself. He loves basketball and God. She prayed he wasn't too good to be true. She wanted someone like him in her life.

Jaylen took his hand off of her shoulder and pulled his long sleeves up to his elbows. Tattooed on his arm was the scripture, 1 John 4:19. Kelly immediately recognized the scripture as it was one of her favorites.

She pointed at his tattoo and said, "We love because He first loved us."

"Yes ma'am. I got this tattoo to remind me of God's love. And every time I see the combo of 4:19 together, whether it's the date or time or if I just glance down at my arm, I am always reminded of this scripture and that Jesus is always there and gets me through everything. It also reminds me my identity can only be found in Jesus alone; not through a career, a hobby, or another person. The problem is we as humans occasionally misconstrue the gifts God blesses us with. The Deceiver will twist the gifts that God gave you and make them into something they are not — look at the Garden of Eden and the fall of man. Satan made them question their identity. That's exactly what he still does today. He makes you question who you are and who you belong to. If we do not root our identity and build our foundation on Jesus, Satan will continue to find ways to attack your identity. It is a tale as old as time...literally."

It suddenly all clicked for Kelly. She had associated the combination of 4 and 19 as something horrible for so long. It reminded her of the pain she felt when she was fired. Jaylen helped her realize God was changing her bad into good. In a completely uncharacteristic move, she grabbed Jaylen with no hesitation and hugged him tightly.

"Thank you," she said.

Jaylen hugged her back, understanding this was not a chance meeting. "I guess it's evident we were both supposed to be here tonight. God's pretty awesome like that."

Kelly leaned back slightly from Jaylen, smiling. As he smiled back, his dimples surfaced. There was something about his grin—effortless and warm—that made her heart soften. But then she snapped back to the reality they were the only two patrons left in the bistro. It was well past closing time.

"Oh my goodness, I'm so sorry," Kelly said to the bartender. "We are keeping you here."

Jaylen leaned over and put his hand on Kelly's arm. "It's okay, I know the owner. He'll take care of her."

"Oh, you know the owner, huh?" Kelly asked.

"Yeah, I'm sorry I didn't mention that before, but my brother-in-law is the owner. I was really enjoying our conversation, and I didn't want to take away from that by any means," he said.

"Oh, your brother-in-law?" Kelly asked with angst. Great, he's married, she thought.

"Yeah, my big sister's husband. He's a great guy. I'm single...in case you were wondering," Jaylen winked.

Kelly breathed a sigh of relief. Jaylen paused for a minute. He turned away, took in a deep breath, and turned back around to Kelly with a very serious look on his face.

"Kelly, I know we just met, but I feel like I need to say this to you. You didn't fail God. I think it is hard for us sometimes to realize, perhaps, you were never meant to see the harvest. Maybe you were just the one who was supposed to plant the seed."

"It's funny you say that. My best friend Peyton, has often used this exact analogy. We always talk about planting the seeds."

"Since you seem to be a basketball connoisseur, I'm assuming you have seen the movie, *The Mighty Macs*?" Jaylen asked.

"Yes, I love that movie!" Kelly said excitedly.

Jaylen continued. "There is a great quote in the movie, 'if we didn't have to struggle, we would never harvest the glory.' Remember that."

Kelly nodded in agreement to the quote. "I can't thank you enough for listening tonight. I needed this. Thank you, Jaylen."

"Anytime, Kelly," Jaylen replied. "We should meet up for coffee sometime or maybe watch some March Madness together. May I put my number in your phone?"

Kelly handed him her phone. It was obvious there was chemistry and a connection between them. If anything, she was hoping to build a friendship with him and see where things went from there.

"Are you sure you can handle watching a game with me," Kelly said. "I'm a bit of a competitive psychopath."

Jaylen grinned at her and simply said, "good."

Kelly said goodbye, thanked him again for listening, and headed for the door.

"Hey, don't give up completely on basketball, but also don't let it control you. Enjoy it the way God intended. That's my last piece of advice for the evening," Jaylen giggled.

"Thank you. I won't," Kelly said as she left the bistro.

16

SAVED

The sun vanished from sight as a mass of ominous clouds swept in, casting the lake into a dark shadow. Lightning briefly illuminated the now pitch-black sky. As the wind intensified, swirling and gaining momentum, the lake water pounded heavily on the dock. The relentless motion jarred Kelly making her feel sick to her stomach. Kelly knew this familiar smell of thunderstorms. She was scared to move on the unsteady dock, but knew she needed to reach the shore. She was soaking wet and feeling chilled.

As Kelly stood up, she noticed the swirling wind swept up her basketball. It began rolling towards the edge of the dock. She was afraid it was going to roll straight into the lake and it would be lost forever. Basketball was her most prized possession. It was the tangible representation of the sweat, struggle, and joy she poured into the sport. It bore the scuff marks of numerous driveway H-O-R-S-E battles, the worn seams from late-night pickup games, and the scars from years of pushing herself to limits she didn't realize she could reach. It was in her hands during her greatest triumphs and her hardest losses. It caught her tears when no one else saw them and gave her purpose when the rest of her world felt uncertain. The thought of losing it felt like losing a part of herself. She went after it exactly how she practiced in high school – diving to the ground and sacrificing her body with total disregard to the cuts and bruises that could arise. No fear. All heart.

"Saved you!" Kelly yelled as she fiercely pulled the basketball toward her, clutching it tightly against her body, right before it rolled off the edge and into the lake. She felt a presence hovering above her. She then heard a familiar faint voice through the swirling wind.

"Kelly, I need you to give me the basketball," the voice said.

"What? No way!" Kelly answered. "This is my basketball. It's my favorite thing in the world. I'm not giving it

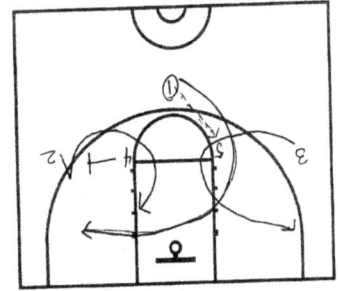

to you. Did you not just see me save it from the lake?" She was already facedown on the dock laying on the basketball, but she continued to clutch it tighter.

"I need you to give it to me," the voice insisted.

"Are you crazy? This isn't yours. It's mine!" Kelly screamed.

Kelly pulled the ball under her body, gripping tighter than she had anything else before.

She then felt a hand gently grab her shoulder. She was anxious and feared this person was trying to steal from her.

"What are you doing? I said NO!" Kelly yelled.

"Kelly, you need to let it go," the faint voice insisted.

She was fearful the hand on her shoulder would grab her violently to wrestle away the ball, but it was the most calming touch she had ever felt. She began to feel peace, but her grip on the basketball was still causing her great anxiety. The basketball began feeling heavier and heavier.

"I don't want anything else. I only want MY basketball," she screamed.

Frustrated, Kelly stood up with her arms wrapped around the basketball. She was ready to fight the person who was trying to steal it. When she turned around, there was no one in sight. She couldn't sense their presence anymore.

She looked around the dock and sprinted to the shore as the thunder and lightning intensified. As she was running, the clouds opened and began dumping buckets of rain upon her. She found it strange she could still see sunshine on the shore. Reaching the shore, it was oddly dry. She heard a second voice.

"Coach, give me the basketball," said the second voice.

This voice had familiarity. "Hello? Who is that? And why do you need THIS basketball?" Kelly replied to this second voice as she looked around the shoreline. A thick fog began rolling across the shore behind Kelly, and she could hardly see anything.

"Kelly, trust me," the original voice said. "It's okay. Give her the ball."

"I can't move forward unless you let go," the second voice said.

Kelly hesitated, her fingers tightening around the basketball she clutched. It embodied who she was—her passion, her purpose, her identity. The weight of the past pressed heavily on her, making the act of surrender seem almost impossible, but the basketball began weighing heavier and heavier. It was becoming almost too heavy for her to hold any longer. She looked down at the basketball, wondering why this was all happening.

As she looked up, fog was engulfing her. She recognized the eyes of the silhouette standing in front of her. "Coach...," the familiar voice said. As she made out the silhouette and paired it with the voice, she could not look away. It was Grace's unwavering gaze. With a deep breath, Kelly extended her arms, offering the basketball to Grace. The moment the ball left her hands, she felt an indescribable lightness. A heavy burden she had carried for too long was released. She expected sadness, but felt relieved instead.

"Trust me, Coach. I'll carry it," Grace whispered.

Kelly was about to ask Grace what she meant by carrying the basketball when she was rocked by a sudden intense blow to her stomach. She jolted awake; it was just Marvin, her cat, trying to wake her up by jumping on her. She was disoriented and confused. As she started to become less groggy, she realized she was in her apartment in Kansas and nowhere near a dock.

She crawled out of bed to feed him and grab some coffee.

"Woah, you scared me, Marvin!" she said aloud to her cat. "You woke your human out of a deep sleep."

Kelly adopted Marvin shortly after she moved back to Kansas after seeing his adorable picture on a shelter's website. A cinnamon and white, fluffy little boy, with an incredibly intelligent personality and sweet, joyful spirit. She called him her angel cat. He became her emotional support.

She got out of bed and staggered to the kitchen. "I haven't had this type of dream in a while. Where did that come from?"

Marvin meowed back at her, patiently awaiting his food.

"Yeah, I don't know either. Here you go, buddy," she said as she placed his food on the ground. "I love you. I hope you know how much joy you bring me. You came into my life when I needed you most…and here I am still carrying on a conversation with a cat."

Marvin continued to chow down on his food. Kelly laughed at herself. She made her coffee and sat down in her recliner before church.

The nightmares of drowning were less frequent, like distant echoes fading into the depths of her mind. The water once symbolized suffocation. Now, the water represented a baptism of sorts—a cleansing allowed her to emerge stronger, wiser, and gave her the ability to move on.

Marvin finished eating and jumped into her lap. As she stroked his velvety fur, she wondered why after five years, she had another dream of the lake. Her involvement with basketball was limited since the day Grace left the court. She figured it was time to grow up and focus on other things in life.

Moving back to Kansas was just what Kelly needed. This move helped her rediscover herself as she interacted with old friends and enjoyed the familiar comforts of 'home.' Not only was she home in the physical sense, but she felt like spiritually she was finally on the path home to her faith in God. Although she stepped away from basketball, she was finding a new purpose in helping a different group of college students and finding healthier work-life balance.

Shortly after they met, Jaylen invited her to attend a local church. Initially hesitant, she felt a persistent tug at her heart to go. The first Sunday she finally accepted Jaylen's invitation, she was uncomfortable. She felt like she needed to be there, but her flesh seemed to fight it. After the beginning of the service worship music, the pastor walked up to the pulpit.

"Today, we are starting a new sermon series that I like to call Chalk Talk," he said. "We are going to examine how sports can teach us about life and God. I'm a former athlete myself, and one lesson I learned from sports is dealing with adversity."

Kelly immediately felt a sense of peace. Out of all the topics the pastor could have chosen, it seemed as though God had crafted this message particularly for her. The pastor told a story about his basketball playing days and overcoming the loss of a state title. Every word resonated with Kelly, making her realize how much she missed her relationship with Jesus.

For years, she had distanced herself from church, always finding excuses: she didn't like the pastor, felt unwelcome, had late-night basketball games, or was too busy planning practices. However, once she began attending with Jaylen, she felt as though each message was directed at her. Gradually, the weight of the past and her pride lifted off her shoulders. She experienced a renewed spirit, a changed heart, and felt her relationship with Jesus growing stronger.

"I'm glad you are here, Kelly. I hope God spoke to you this morning," Jaylen said as he grabbed her hand.

"He definitely did," she said, smiling up at him.

"Will I see you next Sunday?" Jaylen asked.

"Next weekend is my alumni basketball tournament in my hometown, but I'll be back the following Sunday," she said with a smile.

"That's right!" Jaylen said. "Well, I'll see you next Sunday. You'll do great!"

The annual Albany Warriors Basketball Alumni Tournament was Peyton's personal mission to get Kelly to visit home. Even though Kelly moved back to the area years ago, she had not returned to Albany since the Final Four reunion. In some ways, she was still harboring fear of allowing herself to be immersed in basketball culture again and expose her vulnerability in failure.

Peyton badgered Kelly for months to convince her to attend. Eventually, Kelly agreed—on the condition she would reconnect with her former teammates without the pressure to play. The last time she touched a basketball was the last time she was with Grace. Feeling rusty and scared, Kelly hesitated, but Peyton's persistence ultimately persuaded her to lace up her sneakers once again.

"Eye of the Tiger" by Survivor was a constant song on the

pregame playlist during their high school years. Kelly could never quite explain it, but something mentally and physically happened to her when this song began playing. She would become hyper focused and feel as though fire was flowing through her veins. Her teammates would even tease her about it.

"Watch out, y'all! KJ is in her zone," one teammate yelled across the layup line.

"Oh yeah, don't bother her. The other team doesn't know what's coming. Glad we are on her team!" another teammate exclaimed.

"Shut up, guys!" Kelly laughed.

The alumni team Kelly was playing with began warming up.

"Make sure you stretch, ladies. We aren't 17 anymore!" Peyton shouted at the group, and everyone laughed.

KELLY MISSED ALL OF THIS.
SHE MISSED THE CAMARADERIE.
SHE MISSED THE BANTER.
SHE MISSED THE SISTERHOOD.
SHE MISSED HER TEAMMATES AND FRIENDS.
SHE MISSED BASKETBALL.

For the first time in several years—she started to feel a joy she thought she lost.

As they continued stretching and shooting, the gym speakers began blasting "Eye of the Tiger." In the moment, Kelly felt a warm sensation flow through her veins. Her breathing steadied, as it did so many times in past warmups. She closed her eyes and felt the passion for basketball reignite. It was as if she were a teenager again, alone on the basketball court. The fans disappeared, everything became calm and still, and the only sounds were those of her coach and teammates. She was enveloped in a feeling of joy, ecstasy, and power. She felt invincible. No one was going to score on her. It had been 20 years since she experienced this feeling.

The team competed in several games, ultimately securing

the alumni tournament championship. For Kelly, it was like riding a bicycle. As the first game progressed, her years of training kicked in. Her defense was spot on, and she caught fire shooting in the second and third games, ultimately earning the tournament MVP. Championships were nothing new for this squad; winning was ingrained in them. As they celebrated their victory, community members approached the team, congratulating them and expressing gratitude for coming back home to play and putting on a show.

"Y'all were always so fun to watch. We missed this team. You brought so much joy to the community. Thank you for coming back to play," one elderly lady said to Kelly.

"Thank you for coming to watch. I missed us, too," Kelly grinned and replied to the fan.

"How did that feel, KJ?" Peyton asked.

"Like healing," Kelly responded in relief.

"That's what I love to hear, friend!" Peyton exclaimed as she burst Kelly's bubble and gave her a hug.

"Thanks, Pey. I needed this," Kelly whispered as she hugged Peyton back tightly.

"As always, you are welcome. I'm so glad you are here. We all are. Hey! You know, the other day, I thought about the playbook; the one I gave you years ago. Hopefully, it helped you," Peyton winked at Kelly.

Kelly's smile quickly faded into an expression of guilt. "Actually, Peyton. It did, but I hate to tell you this...I lost it a long, long time ago."

"What do you mean?" Peyton asked.

"When I had the falling out with Grace, I was so upset, I threw it. You know how my temper can sometimes get the best of me. That was years ago. It's gone forever now. I'm so sorry," Kelly dropped her head.

Peyton put her hand on Kelly's shoulder. "It's just an object, KJ. It wasn't about the actual playbook. It was about the principles. And look, you are living them!"

"Really? You think so?" Kelly questioned.

"Absolutely. If anything, you took care of the R., I., and the S. today. You rediscovered who you are, you ignited your passion again, and you are strengthening your support system. Now all you have to do is to EMPOWER someone else."

"I like that. You're the best, Peyton," Kelly said. "God certainly blessed me with an amazing best friend. Thank you for putting up with me through all of this and never giving up on me, even when I was kind of miserable to be around."

"I always got you, KJ!" Peyton replied.

After a long day of games, Kelly and her teammates went out to dinner. They talked about the day's games, laughing at funny moments, while also reminiscing about their high school days.

"So KJ, we heard you met a guy," one of her former teammates teased.

"Ha Ha. Y'all are funny. Yes, I did meet someone, but we are just taking the friendship route ..for now. Don't get overly excited," Kelly retorted while blushing.

"Sure...just friends, huh?" another teammate teased.

"Lies! KJ, you like this guy!" another teammate exclaimed.

Kelly began to get a little flustered and embarrassed, just like she did in high school when they would poke fun at her about crushes and typical teenage girl stuff.

"We are just giving you a hard time, KJ, because we love you. We want you to have some joy. And if your friendship with this guy brings you joy, then awesome. If it is more than you are confessing to us," Peyton said while emphatically winking at Kelly, "then that's great, too. If not, we just hope God guides you to give your heart joy, peace, and love. That's all."

"Yeah, KJ, we're just messing with you," a teammate said. "We missed you and this. You need to come back home more often."

"I'll try," Kelly said. "And you're right. I do like this guy."

"Oooohhhhhh!" they all collectively yelled, then laughed.

"C'mon, y'all! Stop!" Kelly laughed. "I have to keep my tough, independent woman image."

After dinner, the team said their goodbyes to one another. Peyton stuck around a little longer to talk to Kelly.

The next morning Kelly met Peyton for brunch. After enjoying some extra time together it was time to say farewell.

"Aren't you glad you came?" Peyton asked.

"I really am, Pey," Kelly replied. "Thanks for never giving up on me. You are an absolute blessing."

"Well, you are, too," Peyton said as she gave her longtime friend a hug goodbye. "Don't forget you are a light. We'll see you at the next one, right?"

"Yes, you will," Kelly hugged back.

As Kelly departed and began her drive back to Kansas, a wave of nostalgia drew her toward a place she hadn't thought of in years. Instead of heading straight home, she steered her car down a familiar road. This road led to the outdoor basketball court, where she had spent countless hours as a child. Memories of dribbling under the hot summer sun and racing against her own competitiveness flooded her mind. Pulling into the gravel lot, she stepped out of her car and paused. The court looked different from her last visit. Fresh paint revitalized the cracked asphalt, once overgrown with weeds and faded lines. A sturdy rim and new nets, which gently moved in the breeze, replaced the rusty hoop. It was as if time had revived a piece of her past.

Kelly walked slowly to the center of the court, the cool breeze brushing against her skin, carrying with it the faint chirping of birds in the nearby trees. What could only be described as an act of God, she discovered an old basketball resting near the edge of the court. She began to shoot. The rhythm of the ball bouncing and swishing through the net was meditative, transporting her back to a simpler time.

A cloud drifted over the sun, sending gentle rays of light streaming down to the court. Kelly paused and gazed upward toward the sky. In the stillness, she felt it—an overwhelming presence of peace, a divine reassurance. It was as though the Holy Spirit was meeting her there on the court, reminding her she was never alone, even in the moments of uncertainty and devastation.

Kelly stayed a little longer, savoring the tranquility she felt playing as a little girl. When she finally got back into her car, she glanced one last time at the place that shaped her. She grinned and whispered, "Thank you," and she drove away, feeling lighter, as if some unspoken burden had been lifted.

The road ahead seemed brighter now, not just with the promise of home but with the hope that every detour, every unexpected stop along life's path, carried its own quiet miracles.

17

EMPOWER

More than a decade passed since Grace last stepped foot on the basketball court she found on the day of her grandmother's funeral. She could not believe how fast time had elapsed. The last time she stood on the court was the day she graduated with her undergraduate degree. She stood alone, wondering where life was going to take her. At this time in her life, everything seemed bleak.

"Wow, I can't believe how long it has been since I was here last," Grace said to her personal assistant, Julie.

"How long has it been, boss?" Julie asked.

"Well, since my life changed," Grace said as she smiled and turned towards Julie. "I was a 22-year-old, scared kid. I stood right in this very spot and prayed. It's crazy how much I remember from that day."

Grace looked up at the sky and felt a little emotional. She looked down and tried to gather herself before speaking to Julie. She did not want to break down. Today was a day to be celebrated.

"I have a lot of memories from this place. And now here we are," Grace said.

"Well, boss, congratulations! You have earned it. And think of all those kids you are going to help," Julie replied, grinning ear-to-ear.

"Thank you," Grace said. "A long time ago, my college basketball coach said to me to 'be the person you needed when you were younger.' So, it's what I'm trying to do. This is the perfect place for the initiative to begin. And the building...well, it looks terrific!"

Grace and Julie walked around the court. It was no longer rundown like it was during Grace's college years. It was a newly renovated outdoor court, with new lighting, benches and a brand new building adjacent to it. The new building included an indoor basketball court, a recreation room, a food pantry, offices for counselors, and a large

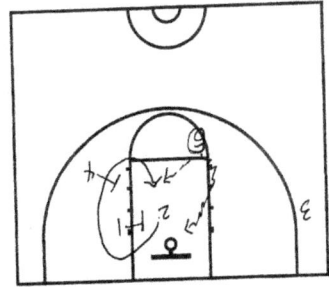

community room. There was a distinct charm in the outdoor court, and even more so with its revitalization. When the land went to auction a couple of years prior, Grace could not pass on the opportunity to bid on it. Acquiring this land was the perfect place to open a basketball academy building. It was a labor of love taking shape over numerous years.

The night Grace and Kelly had their falling-out at the outdoor court, Grace drove around until dawn. She found herself crying out to God, pleading with Him to take away her pain. As the sunrise approached, she pulled into a parking lot. She cracked her windows and drifted off to sleep. After what only felt like a few minutes but was actually a couple of hours, she woke up to the sound of cars entering the parking lot. The sun was shining on a sign of a small church that read "morning service at 8:00 a.m. and 10:30 a.m." It was Sunday at nearly 8:00 a.m. Before she knew it, she was suddenly getting out of her car and walking into the church. She slipped into the Harvest Bible Church's sanctuary and sat in the back pew. She sat there motionless, absorbing the worship music, the sermon, the scriptures, and the prayers. Near the end of the service, she got up to sneak out and bumped into a gentleman in the lobby. The gentleman was standing by a table with a stack of bibles. He handed her one, and wished her God's blessings. She didn't say anything in return but clutched the bible in her hand and walked out the door. She sat in her car numb. She opened her new bible to a random page and began reading.

```
"For I know the plans I have for you,"
declares the LORD, "plans to prosper you and
not to harm you, plans to give you hope and
a future. You will seek me and find me when
you seek me and find me with all your heart.
I will be found by you," declares the LORD,
"and will bring you back from captivity."
(Jeremiah 29:11-14)
```

Grace sobbed. Jeremiah 29:11 was on a piece of wall art hanging in Nana's home, but Grace never cared to understand it. She passed by this scripture nearly daily for years. This was the first time reading it she felt the presence of God. She started reading more about Jesus, trying to understand who He was. Earlier in the summer she was contemplating suicide, but now she wanted to live. She prayed and asked God to forgive and save her. She wanted to make an impact on others. In an unexpected way, she now had hope.

She decided it would be in her best interest to finish out her senior year by taking all of her courses online. Luckily, Lions Park University offered all of the courses she needed as online options. She found a job to support herself while she finished her degree. She was determined to prove the world wrong.

At her graduation ceremony, Grace looked for Coach Janssen. She was disappointed when she discovered Kelly wasn't in attendance. Her feelings of anger and abandonment resurfaced.

A couple months later, she found Kelly's graduation card buried under a pile of junk mail in Nana's house as she was preparing to move and sell the house. After reading the card, she felt guilty for her actions and for still harboring resentment towards Kelly. She knew she should reach out, but pride held her back. Instead, she buried her feelings, moved on, and shifted her focus to her next chapter of life.

After Grace graduated with her undergraduate degree in business, she took a chance and pursued a MBA (Masters in Business Administration). To help with her tuition payments, she worked at The Lee Sports Center, a nearby sports facility. There she officiated basketball games, serving as a scorekeeper, and picking up any other types of odd jobs she could find to help pay her bills. While working there, she met an elderly man, a grandfather-like figure, who had a passion for youth sports. He had inherited a fortune and loved investing in others and his community. He was the owner and founder of the sports facility. She did not realize who he was when she first met him. He enjoyed discretely stopping by periodically to check on his facility. His favorite sport was basketball, so he would try to take in a few games while he was there.

The facility just hosted one of their largest basketball showcases for high school prospects of the fall. Hundreds of teams, families, and college coaches filled the facility from dawn to dusk for four days straight. Grace refereed her last game of Sunday evening after being there all weekend. She came off the court exhausted, but noticed there was a spill on the floor. Without any hesitation, she keyed into a maintenance closet, pulled out a mop, and began cleaning up the mess. The man walked over to her as she cleaned.

"What's your name, young lady," he said as he walked towards her. There were very few people left in the building, but Grace was still surprised when he addressed her.

"Me? My name is Grace. May I help you with something, sir?" Grace replied.

"You seem like you really put a lot of care into your work," he replied back. "Your parents taught you well."

"Oh," Grace said with hesitation. "Thank you, but credit goes to my Nana."

"I see. Grandmothers are truly a blessing from God," he responded.

Grace was not sure where this conversation was heading, but the gentleman seemed quite determined to carry on talking to her.

"Are you in college?" he asked.

"Yes, sir. I'm working on my MBA," Grace replied.

"That's terrific. What are your plans with your degree?" he questioned.

Grace giggled. "Honestly, sir. I'm not quite sure yet. I just felt led to get it, like it would open some doors for my future."

"Well, that's good you are pursuing it then. I think many times in life we don't listen to the voice directing our steps. So, it is very good you are listening to it."

"Yeah, I guess so," Grace said hesitantly as she continued to mop up the spill. "Thank you. Are you sure I cannot help you with something, sir?"

"Thank you, but I am okay. However, I think maybe I can help you," he said. "What are your dreams and goals, Grace?"

Grace paused for a minute. The man could tell she was hesitant to open up.

"Okay, let me rephrase this question," he continued. "If you had all of the resources at your disposal and knew you could not fail, what would you do in life?"

"Wow, that's quite a question, sir. Well, if I had all of the resources I needed and knew I couldn't fail, I would definitely do something with basketball to help kids. To help kids like me," Grace responded.

"Now we are talking," the man said.

As the conversation continued, Grace learned the gentleman she was speaking to was Thomas Lee, the owner and founder of The Lee Center. They had an in depth conversation, and Mr. Lee continued to visit the facility for several weeks to check in on Grace. He was so impressed with her work ethic, kindness, intelligence, communication skills, and internal drive, he offered her a position as an Executive Assistant, reporting directly to him. Mr. Lee felt led to help her, and he told her it was a divine sign they met.

Grace worked as an executive assistant for Mr. Lee for several years, even staying on with his company after completing her MBA. He had no direct descendants and treated Grace in some aspects, almost like his granddaughter. He gave her many opportunities to gain knowledge in the business side of sports and taught her valuable lessons in investing in the community. Grace took all his advice and knowledge to heart. He taught her to put away a little seed money with each paycheck, even if it was only a small amount. Mr. Lee saw a lot of similarities between himself and Grace, and when he thought she was ready, he invested in her financially to begin making her dream come true.

After a year of construction, the basketball academy's grand opening neared. Grace was in town for the ribbon cutting ceremony. Her plan was to open more academies across the country. She was very emotional as she realized how far she had come.

Unfortunately, Mr. Lee had passed away before construction began on her project. He always told her he believed in her. She told him she wanted to name the academy after him, but he insisted she did not. "This is your dream. I'm just a small part of your story," he always said to her.

As Grace reflected, she thought about the people in her life who truly believed in her: Trey, Nana, Mr. Lee, and Coach Janssen. She thought about Coach Janssen often. She was disappointed they had not spoken since their falling out so many years ago. Grace had finally let go of all her demons, and she knew she needed to contact her coach. She knew Coach Janssen wouldn't be the first to reach out to her because she knew Kelly wasn't going to force the relationship. Grace was embarrassed about how she had acted the last day she saw Kelly. She was ashamed so much time had passed. It was something she just kept putting off.

"Where to next, boss?" Julie asked.

"That's a great question, Julie," Grace laughed as they were opening their car doors.

Just then the architect ran towards the two yelling, "Ms. Villanueva! Wait!"

"Ms. Villanueva!" he yelled until Grace responded.

"Yes?"

"I'm so glad I caught you. I forgot to give this to you" he said as he handed Grace what looked like a very beat up, old, booklet.

"What is this?" Grace asked.

"I don't know, but it has a picture of you in it," the architect said.

"What?" Grace opened the journal and realized what she was holding.

"Oh my goodness," she gasped. "Where did you...how...I ...I can't believe this!"

"What is it, boss?" Julie asked.

"It's the playbook," Grace explained. "I can't believe it. I thought I would never see this again. Long story short, it was my coach's, and we had this falling out...and I threw it at her...where did you get this? Did my coach give it to you?"

"No, ma'am," the architect said. "When the contractors were excavating the court, they found it. The head foreman saved it and said I needed to give it to you. He thought the drawing in it looked like you from the photo you gifted to the building. The college photograph where you are shooting a layup, I believe. He thought you would get a kick out of it. But wow, I didn't realize you actually had a connection to it."

Tears began streaming down Grace's face. The architect excused himself, and Grace and Julie got into the car. Grace stared at the playbook, opening it, turning pages, and repeating this action again and again. A few of the pages were stuck together, but the lessons were all there. She was shocked it was still legible and only the outside of the journal appeared to be damaged. Grace shared with Julie about the summer Nana passed away and how Coach Janssen tried to help her. She told her how they never finished the lesson of R.I.S.E.

"How far did you get?" Julie asked.

"Well, not far enough." Grace turned to the "E" lesson and read it to Julie.

E: Empower others.

Finally, when we were near the end of the season, Coach always told us to trust ourselves and each other. She took a step back and just let us play. Why did Coach say and do this? As a 17-year-old kid, I didn't get what she was doing. As I look back now, I understand Coach reiterated this point because she was empowering us to take control of our destiny on the court. By this point in the season, she already trained us and taught us what we needed to know to be successful, but ultimately, we had to go perform.

One of the hardest things as a coach or a mentor is letting go. As much as we as coaches would love to take those hard falls, losses, failures, bumps, and bruises for our players, we can't go play the game for them. You can't go out there and live life for your kids. You are not always going to be in a position to have a timeout to save them. You try your best to teach them all that you can so they learn to trust their training. You try to empower those in your care to take control of their destiny to be successful in life. You do your best to prepare them for battle in this world.

This is why I know you coached. It's bigger than basketball. Don't be afraid of your own voice. God has called us to plant the seeds. Your gifts of empathy and belief are attributes that make you powerful with your words. You've been placed in these young people's lives to make a difference and to pay it forward. How do we do this? We know our role and we buy into it. We love them, and we prepare them. Because the truth of the matter is, you can't play the game of life for them. You don't have timeouts in life to save them when they are in trouble. And sometimes, you have to let them fail to learn and grow. We want to see them succeed, so we do our best to teach them skills that we have learned along the way. We know how hard life is. We want to make sure they are ready and equipped for all of the challenges they will face and to help them become the best they can be.

Great teams are successful because they trust and empower each other. Think about a basketball game. Beautiful basketball occurs when a team works together

as one, seamlessly moving the ball on offense where
everyone on the court gets a touch. Coach reiterated
this often. A team that tallies numerous assists in a
game puts themselves in a position to be successful.
Not only does this create efficient basketball, but it
empowers your teammates. The unselfish act of passing
up on a shot to give your teammate a moment of glory
for a better shot is...well...glorious. Each team member
has a special skill set to bring to the team. No need
to be envious or become jealous of each other. A great
team simply supports each other towards a common goal.

What is the ultimate goal as a coach? To serve your
players by empowering them to apply those skills as a
warrior and RISE when adversity strikes. Empowering
them will give them the confidence in the future to
empower others in their future.

Empower Others:

1. Know and buy into your role.
    •You are unique.
    •You have unique gifts that contribute to the
    team's success.

2. Pay it forward.
    •Serve others.
    •Think outside of yourself.

3. Help your teammates become the best they can be.
    •Plant the seeds. You may never see the
    harvest, but plant the seeds anyway.
    •Encouragement breeds confidence.
    •Don't be afraid of your own voice.

•Your vulnerability will help others RISE by
creating trust and connection.

Grace in shock spoke under her breath, "I can't believe this. After all of these years. Wow."

"That's really ironic, boss," Julie stated.

Grace was choked up. She took a deep breath, and looked over at Julie.

"It's no irony. It's a miracle," Grace said.

"Doesn't this all kind of feel like a sign? Like it's time to contact your coach," Julie reiterated.

"Yes, 100 percent. But first, I just had a revelation we need to make happen."

18

THE COMEBACK

Kelly was preparing for her Easter weekend trip to visit her parents. Axel and Anne relocated to the Lake of the Ozarks years ago to enjoy their retirement. Though her mom's health was still deteriorating, they found joy in their retirement village. Kelly expected a serene weekend with them. As she completed her packing, memories flooded back from the year her life took a pivotal turn.

There were moments when it was hard for Kelly to grasp just how many years had slipped by since this chapter of her life. Memories from that time did not surface as often now, but every so often, a wave of sadness would still wash over her. She had stepped away from coaching entirely, a decision she made to focus on her own healing.

And then Jaylen walked into her life. Meeting him rekindled her love for basketball, a spark she thought had faded. They often watched and attended basketball games together. He had even convinced her to help out once in a while with the youth team he was coaching. One baby step at a time, but he was determined to rekindle the fire within her. What started as a chance encounter grew into a deep friendship and evolved into something romantic. Jaylen became her accountability partner in her walk with God, a steady presence with the heart of a servant leader, always offering his help. For Kelly, fiercely self-reliant, letting someone else in was unfamiliar territory. Accepting his support was difficult—but she was still learning to let him in.

"Do you have everything?" Jaylen asked, as he grabbed a piece of her luggage.

"I think so," Kelly said.

They both walked out the door carrying her luggage to her car.

"I'm sorry I can't come with you tomorrow, but I'll make sure I'm there Sunday," Jaylen said. "Not all of us get the luxury of Good Friday off in this evil world."

He smirked at her, as he

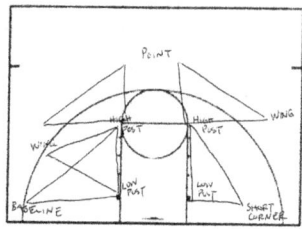

grabbed the bag from her hand to load her car.

"I could have done that myself," she said.

"Oh, I know you are more than capable," he retorted back. "But it is also okay to let other people help you."

"Fine," she said as she smiled back at him. "And it is okay you won't be there until Sunday. Just means more of my mom's fried chicken for me."

She winked at him.

"That's brutal, Kel. Your mom loves me, so I'm sure I can convince her to make more on Sunday. Like you and your dad would be upset," he said sarcastically as he started walking inside. "Oh, the joys of having to work on Good Friday." The moment he said Good Friday, Kelly suddenly remembered the fateful Friday. She stopped and stood outside for a few moments.

"Are you okay?" Jaylen asked as he turned around and noticed she had spaced off.

"I'm fine," she said as her mind continued to wander. "Hey, can you give me a few minutes alone?"

"Yeah," Jaylen replied. "Are you sure you are okay?"

"I just need a minute," she replied.

Jaylen was well aware it was Good Friday and the significance of the day to Kelly. He slowly walked over to her, gave her a kiss on the cheek, and said, "No problem. Take your time. I love you."

"Thank you," she said as she softly smiled at him. "I love you, too."

Kelly reflected on the multitude of lessons gleaned from Good Friday. Although she lost *The R.I.S.E. Playbook* years ago, Kelly recalled Peyton talking about The Comeback. Every great, inspiring sports story has a story of adversity and a story of an epic comeback. It had taken Kelly quite some time to fully grasp the storm she endured and ultimately strengthened her. She pondered whether she had truly left an imprint on her former athletes' lives or if they had absorbed any wisdom from her. She sat down on the stairs outside of her apartment. She reached in her pocket, grabbed her phone, and journaled in the notes section, she began doing this often after reading the playbook.

The Comeback

One of the most difficult experiences I've ever gone
through was my ACL injury. I remember when I tore it,
I was in denial of what happened. I convinced myself
that, at worst, it was just a torn meniscus. It wasn't.
The injury I dreaded the most as an athlete inevitably
happened. I was dealing with an injury I wouldn't wish
on my worst rival. I experienced a lot of injuries
in my time as an athlete. The physical aspect of the
injury I can handle. But the mental strain of an ACL
injury is nothing anyone can prepare you for. It
challenges you mentally in ways you cannot imagine.
And unless you have experienced this injury, it's hard
to really understand what it is like to go through the
healing process.

But the one thing I learned from this experience
was how mentally tough I actually was. Surgery, weeks
of being on crutches, and the months upon months of
rehabilitation tested every ounce of my being. But as
I always did as an athlete, I put my head down and
continued to go to work. I was consistent in completing
my exercises, even when it was unbearably painful.
It was a long road, and yes, sometimes incredibly
frustrating. There are moments you want to give up
because in the beginning, you don't see the progress
immediately. Like overcoming any adversity in life, it
takes time. I would have days when I felt great and
imagined I would be cleared sooner than later, only to
wake up the next day, barely able to bend my stiff knee.
And in those moments when it seems like all this work
and mental strain is a waste of time, stay mentally
strong and keep going.

Overcoming adversity and making a comeback are

like the healing and recovery process of an ACL injury. It's grueling, it tests you, and it takes a lot of mental toughness. Life is hard, and like Peyton once said to me, sometimes you have to just survive and advance. As it is said in Romans 5:3-4, "Not only so, but we also glory in our sufferings, because we know that suffering produces perseverance; perseverance, character; character, hope." In this painful season, I focused on the little victories. I focused on the positives. I thanked God for the experience because I knew someday it would also give me an avenue to help someone else.

We go through these painful, challenging, experiences because the process refines us and builds resiliency. I've never been a fan of the saying "God never gives more than you can handle." That's not true. I think He allows us to experience these things because we learn we can't do this life alone, and we need to lean on and rely on Him. Like the Footprints poem, the man only saw one set of footprints during the most challenging storms because the Lord carried him through the toughest parts of life. And when we overcome adversity and make an epic comeback, we are a testament to others. "I can do all things through Christ who strengthens me." - Philippians 4:13

Like we always said as a team when we were trailing in a game, you can't come back from a 20-point deficit with one, single shot. Comebacks are a process. Make the most of each offensive and each defensive possession. You must value each possession and live in the moment. Like basketball, comebacks in life are a process. You have to live in the present and take it one moment and one day at a time.

I wish I would have told myself this years ago

when I faced my coaching storm. I would have saved
myself years of grief, but maybe I needed a reminder
that a setback is just the setup for an epic comeback.
I'm proud of myself for all I've overcome in this
life. I'm proud of my growth as a person and the
growth in my relationship with Jesus. Now, I can use
these different seasons of adversity for good, and I
know how to RISE and to help others RISE.

To execute an epic comeback story, remember:

• Comebacks are a process.
• There will be setbacks.
• Value each possession.

• Survive and Advance.
• Renew your soul and face the storm head on.
• Jesus will carry you.

It may be painful at times, but the process is worth
who you become because of the storm you experienced.

As she finished journaling and placed her phone back into
her pocket, her mind continued wandering to thoughts of basketball.
There would often be moments which triggered memories of her
former players or prompted thoughts about their well-being. While she
remained in touch with some, others had slipped out of her reach, their
only connection being social media follows. However, one athlete was
on her mind frequently... Grace.

Just as she snapped back to reality, her phone started vibrating
in her pocket. The number was unfamiliar, and she usually ignored
calls from unknown numbers. But something urged her to answer this
call.

"This is Kelly," she answered.

"Coach!" the voice exclaimed. "Is it really you?!" the voice questioned.

"Well, no one has really called me coach in years, but this is Kelly Janssen. Is that who you are looking for? I'm sorry, but who is this?"

"Coachhhh!!! C'mon. You know who this is," the voice on the other end giggled. "Coach, it's Grace."

After sending Grace the graduation letter and never receiving a response, Kelly never imagined she would ever hear from her again, but perhaps she should have known. After all, Grace kept coming to her mind a lot in recent weeks. It was almost as if God was trying to tell her something. Kelly was ecstatic when she realized it was Grace's voice.

"Grace?!" Kelly exclaimed. "What?! Oh my goodness! It's so good to hear your voice. How are you? Where are you? What are you up to?!"

"It's so good to hear your voice too, Coach," Grace said. "I'm doing well. I'm...I guess you can say 'around.' How are you? Is it okay if I still call you Coach?"

"I'm good. And, yes, of course. I'm happy to hear you even want to call me Coach," Kelly sighed. "Grace, I'm so sorry..."

"I'm going to stop you right there, Coach," Grace interrupted. "You have nothing to be sorry for. If anything, I do. But, let's save that conversation for another time because I'm actually calling to share something with you. I'm hoping we could have an opportunity to meet up in person."

"Sure, Grace. In person? Really? What's up? When?" Kelly responded.

"Wow, all the rapid-fire questions. Are you still in Kansas?" Grace asked.

"Yes, I am," Kelly responded.

"Well, I have a surprise for you. Do you think you could meet me tomorrow? I know this is last minute, but it's important," Grace said.

"Tomorrow? As in Good Friday?" Kelly questioned.

"Yes, Good Friday," Grace giggled. "I've been so busy and

186

excited, I kind of blanked tomorrow is Good Friday. Well then...now this is perfect."

"What are you up to, Grace? I was actually heading to my parents' place for Easter at the Lake of the Ozarks, but I could leave a little later. Wait, are you in Kansas?"

"I will be in the Kansas City area tomorrow. That's not far from you, right? Please, Coach. I hate to ask you to take time away from your family, but I really need to see you and I really need you to see this. Would you be able to go at 10:00 a.m.?"

"Yeah, Kansas City is only 20 to 40 minutes away from where I live, depending where you want to meet. I can do 10."

"Awesome, Coach! How are your parents?!"

"They are doing pretty well. I mean, my mother has her usual ailments, but honestly, they are doing okay. Thank you so much for asking."

"Of course! They were always supportive of me, so I'm glad they are well. Well, I hate to cut this short, but I have to run to a meeting. Trust me, you are not going to regret this. AHHH! I'm so excited. I'll text you the address. This is a comeback of epic proportions. You just wait. Love you, Coach!"

"Awe. I love you, too, Grace! I've missed you."

"I've missed you, too. And thank you for letting me still call you coach because you will always be my coach. Can't wait to see you. See you tomorrow!"

"See you tomorrow, Grace," Kelly said before ending the call.

Kelly stood in front of her apartment, stunned. After all these years, she was finally going to be reunited with Grace. She wondered where life had taken her, what she was doing now, and how she would react to seeing her again. At least over the phone, Grace sounded in great spirits. This warmed Kelly's heart.

"Who was that?" Jaylen asked as Kelly walked back into the apartment.

"One of my former players I haven't spoken to in probably ten years," Kelly paused. "You know, I never told you this, but I've had this recurring dream for years about drowning in a lake."

"That sounds awful," Jaylen replied. "Enlighten me again on how this has anything to do with your former player?"

"J...," she said, giving him a look as he flirtatiously smiled back at her.

"I'm just giving you a hard time, Kel. Please proceed."

"Thank you. Where I was going with this is since I was a kid, I would have this recurring nightmare I was drowning in the lake. I assumed it was probably because of the Lake of the Ozarks, and I almost fell in when I was little. In my adult years, especially when I lost my coaching position, I started having these recurring dreams. Right before I went home for the alumni tournament, I had the dream again."

"Okay, so you had a dream you were drowning. Well, that makes sense with everything you told me you experienced," Jaylen responded. "But can you elaborate?"

"Yes, of course. I would dream I would be in the lake, just feet from the dock. And I would get pulled under the water. It felt like someone grabbed my ankle and pulled me under. But sometimes, I would see a light above the water, a hand would grab my arm and pull me out, and then I would wake up. But the last time I had the dream, it was different. I was on the dock, and I had a basketball I didn't want to let go of and this one voice kept telling me to let HER have it. The 'her' was Grace!"

"Oh, so God was telling you that you planted the seeds in Grace. Now let her grow?"

"Why are you so irritating?" Kelly laughed.

Jaylen smiled back at her, walked over to her, and hugged her. "Because God knew you needed someone to keep you humble."

He slowly pulled away and winked at her while clutching both of her hands.

"In all seriousness, Kel. It's the season of miracles. Maybe you get to see the harvest after all. And I would bet the crops will overwhelm you."

19

RISS

I t was a twist of fate, or possibly divinely orchestrated. Good Friday landed again on April 19. But this time, the atmosphere was charged with a different energy. It wasn't just another Good Friday; it was a day brimming with celebration and anticipation. The sky was clear, not a single cloud in sight, and the sun beamed down brightly. Kelly felt as though her prodigal daughter was finally returning home.

She finished packing her car, and typed in the address Grace sent her into her maps app. Following the navigation, she wondered what "surprise" Grace had in store. She pulled up to an industrial area. Sitting on the corner of 3rd Avenue and Cornerstone Road was an old, rundown, abandoned church. Kelly pulled over on the side of the street in front of the church to confirm the information Grace had texted her. She thought maybe her GPS had taken her on the wrong route. As she was looking down at her phone, there was suddenly a tap on the driver's side car window.

Startled, Kelly looked up at a familiar face and rolled down her window.

"Grace!" Kelly exclaimed.

"Hi, Coach," Grace said with a huge grin on her face.

Kelly quickly unfastened her seatbelt, swung open her car door, jumped out of the car and nearly tackled Grace to give her a hug.

"It's so good to see you, Coach," Grace said as she hugged her back.

"What are you doing here? What is this? Where are we?" Kelly asked Grace as she stared up at the building.

"Woah with the rapid-fire questions again, Coach," Grace giggled. "You sound like me! Well, I wanted you to see my passion project, Coach." She

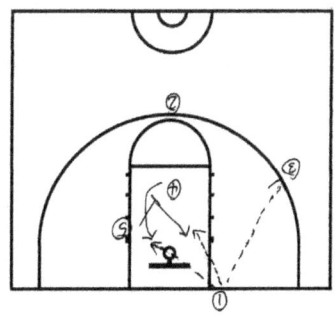

looked across at the church, pointing at the rundown building.

"Okay?" Kelly said in confusion. "What is it?"

"Well, Coach," Grace said sarcastically. "It's obviously a run down, old church. But it isn't what it is, but what it will be, which is a basketball academy."

She paused for a moment, looked at Kelly, and winked. "Well, we are calling this facility The Warriors RIS3 Basketball Chapel. It's a place of community, dedication and personal growth. I want to help kids find a sense of purpose and focus, aligning with the idea basketball is more than a sport—it's a passion, a calling and a resource. We are going to support kids by providing a basketball development program, scholarships, mental health support, and more. I guess you can say those who believed in me inspired me. This will be our second location. The first one is at our basketball court, Coach, where you brought church to me. I want to do the same for others."

Grace pulled out her phone and showed Kelly pictures of the first basketball "sanctuary," the renovated court, the ribbon-cutting and opening ceremonies. She explained she immediately researched purchasing an area to build the same type of facility near Kelly.

"You named it WARRIORS RISE?!" Kelly asked. "I'm speechless, Grace. This is so cool and so perfect for you."

"Yes, Coach," Grace said with a smile. "I was listening."

She explained what happened after they had their falling out. They talked for hours in the parking lot, like they did so many times after practices and games so many years ago, catching each other up on work, relationships and everything in between.

"Grace, I'm so proud of you," Kelly said. "I don't even know how to tell you how proud I am of you."

"No need to say anything, Coach. You were always there for me, even when we didn't see each other. I can't even tell you how many times in a day I'd say something or was reminded of all the lessons and things I learned from you, Trey, Nana, and my business mentor, Mr. Lee. He was like a guardian angel, honestly. He financially backed me to start all of this. He would have loved you, Coach, and you would have enjoyed his stories. He was like a surrogate grandpa. I thought of you often for all these years, and I guess my pride got the best of me. I should have reached out sooner, but I was honestly embarrassed by my actions. That was such a difficult time in my life, and I just didn't understand a lot of what was happening. I do now. The Holy Trinity is the reason I'm here. Besides the personal significance of it, that's why I added the '3' at the end of RIS3. This is all so much deeper than just the game."

"Well, I'm so happy you seem like you found your joy and your purpose," Kelly replied.

"I did, Coach. I did, and I'm hoping you would help me execute it here. I could use a great basketball coach and mentor."

"It has been a long time since anyone called me coach. I don't know about coaching, but I am definitely here for support."

"God fixes brokenness, Coach. You taught me that. You know, I didn't realize until a few years ago that Dr. Naismith was an ordained pastor and part of the reason he invented basketball was to spread the gospel. I now understand why this game meant so much to both of us."

Grace reached into her pocket and pulled out a tattered, small journal.

"Well, maybe this will change your mind." She handed it to Kelly.

"What is this?" Kelly asked, confused.

"It's the playbook, Coach," Grace said as she handed it to Kelly.

"You are kidding me?! There is no way!" Kelly exclaimed. "I chucked this at the court after we had our little blow up. How did you find it? Did you go back that night?"

"No, Coach," Grace explained. "It was just given to me a few months ago when we were having the ribbon cutting for the first center. Mr. Lee invested in me, so I invested in the place that changed my life. Some contractors found it when they were renovating the area. The picture you gave me in college, the one from your office, is hanging in the center now. I guess they also found this in the back of the playbook and thought it looked like me."

Grace handed Kelly a small, sketched drawing of a female basketball player reaching for a basketball goal in what could be interpreted as fire or water on a basketball court. What appeared to be an arm reaching out of the court trying to grab the player, while another hand was clutched around the player's other ankle.

"That's because it is you," Kelly said. "I didn't even know it was in the playbook. I drew it one night after a dream I had while we were still training."

"Pretty impressive, Coach. I didn't even know you were artistic."

"I mean, I'm not really. I took art in high school and dabbled in sketching in college, but it was just for fun. I had sketched nothing for years, but it was one of those things I had to get out of me."

"I get it, Coach," Grace replied back. "Well, knowing you, there has to be some interpretation to this. Am I right?"

"Yes, Grace," Kelly laughed. "You know me well. I had this recurring dream for years that I was in a lake drowning, when suddenly a hand would grasp my ankle and try to pull me under. But in time, the dream shifted to a hand pulling me out of the water and then I was on a dock, and I think I saw the Lord. Then someone was trying to take my basketball. And eventually, a voice was saying 'trust me,' and to give the basketball to you, actually. Anyway, I just woke up from a dream where I was drowning before one of our training sessions and started sketching," Kelly paused. "I named this sketch 'warriors rise,' actually."

Grace Villanueva, MBA
CEO
The Warriors RIS3
Basketball Foundation

"Raising Warriors On and Off the Court"

"Wait...are you serious?" Grace asked Kelly. Grace reached into her pocket, pulled a business card and handed it to Kelly.

Kelly smiled.

"Well, as you said in my graduation letter, the only explanation for any of this is God," Grace said.

"Yes, and as someone once said to me during a time when I needed to hear it most, 'a true warrior has the heart and perseverance to overcome any obstacle and rise above so they may come out successful and stronger than when they started.' That's you, kiddo," Kelly said.

"Wow, that was deep. I should put that quote on the chapel walls," Grace replied. "Who said it?"

"You."

Kelly winked at Grace. Grace smiled and walked towards Kelly and gave her a hug. "Thank you," she said and handed Kelly a sealed card. "Read it later."

"Of course, Grace," Kelly responded. "You know I'm always here for you. I love you, kiddo."

The two embraced, vowing to see each other again soon. Kelly got in her car. She took a moment to sit in silence before she began her trip to her parents' lake house. She placed the card on the console and began her three hour drive.

In all the excitement of the day, Kelly forgot to fill up her gas tank. She found the nearest gas station. After filling up, she pulled into a parking spot, went inside, bought a drink and a snack, and got back into her car. She took in a deep breath, then exhaled slowly. Before she continued on her journey, she decided to read the card Grace gave her.

Dear Coach,

I don't know if I can ever find the words to thank you enough.

I'm so sorry for everything I said to you the last time I saw you. I was hurt and felt abandoned. I needed to find Jesus, and I think in a weird way I needed to be totally alone to do so. But, Coach, you planted the seed. You are truly a harvester of rising potential.

I know you were devastated when you lost your coaching job, but I'm thankful because I don't know I would have gained the faith and resiliency I learned from you otherwise. You may not know why, but I think ALL OF THIS happened for a reason. I hope you understand you're more of a light than you realize for so many people, including myself. He knew I needed someone like you in college and now. Thank you for answering His call.

You will always be someone who changed my life in tremendous ways. You believed in me when I didn't even believe in myself. You saw something in me before I did. You are one of the best people in my life. You are more than just a coach...you are my role model and someone I can count on. Thank you for the tough love and for being one of my biggest supporters.

Everyone has a story, Coach. And sometimes God uses your pain to help others. You taught me that. Maybe it's time for you to share your story and RIS3.

I never told you this, but the day at the outdoor court when I collapsed, you were the answer to my prayer. I wasn't okay. It felt like I was drowning. I didn't want to live, and I was plotting ways to die. I'd never truly prayed before, but in that moment, I had nothing else to lose. It may sound sappy, but God used you to save my life. I fully believe God sent you to pull me out of the water. I love you, Coach. I don't know where I would be without you. You always said, "Be the person you needed when you were younger." You were the person I needed.

I know how much you love your quotes, and I read this quote that immediately made me think of you. I think is important for you to have it right now:

"Sometimes your healed scars are someone else's hope."

If it wasn't for you, I don't know where I would be today.

Love you forever.

One of your "warriors,"
Grace #3

"Wow," Kelly said aloud, wiping tears from her face. She did not know she made this type of an impact on Grace. She had always felt like she let her down when they couldn't continue with their training. After all the years, her dreams also made sense. The divine hand metaphorically pulling her out of the dark waters always had a plan.

She drove a few hours to her parents' house. When she arrived, she updated her parents on Grace and everything that took place on Good Friday. As she was unpacking and her parents were resting, she accidentally knocked her bag over and something fell out onto the floor. She leaned over to pick it up and realized it was *The R.I.S.E. Playbook*. Kelly picked the playbook up and noticed a couple of the pages in the back of the book appeared to be stuck together. As Kelly pulled the pages so gently apart, she noticed something was written inside the back of the book, something she had never noticed before.

"GRACE carried me here, and by GRACE I will carry on."

Kelly realized Peyton had no idea Grace's name when she gave her the book. Grace was right in what she observed. Divine inspiration and intervention were really the only explanations for any of this. Grace said Kelly saved her, but it was by God's "grace" they were both saved.

Kelly opened her Bible and turning to Ephesians:

> As for you, you were dead in your transgressions and sins, in which you used to live when you followed the ways of this world and of the ruler of the kingdom of the air, the spirit who is now at work in those who are disobedient. All of us also lived among them at one time, gratifying the cravings of our flesh and following its desires and thoughts. Like the rest, we were by nature deserving of wrath. But because of his great love for us, God, who is rich in mercy, made us alive with Christ even when we were dead in transgressions—it is by grace you have been saved. And God raised us up with Christ and seated us with him in the heavenly realms in Christ Jesus, in order that in the coming ages he might show the incomparable riches of his grace, expressed in his kindness to us in Christ Jesus. For it is by grace you have been saved, through faith—and this is not from yourselves, it is the gift of God—not by works, so that no one can boast. For we are God's handiwork, created in Christ Jesus to do good works, which God prepared in advance for us to do. (Ephesians 2:1-10, NIV)

Feeling inspired to finally embark on the passion project she always dreamed of, Kelly fired up her laptop and started writing. She smiled, and she realized this was all part of her purpose. She started typing another poem:

RIS3

It was a Good Friday.
A day much like today.
When I felt my heartbeat,
And the bounce came back to play.

The darkness that engulfed me,
Was conquered by a holy trinity.
My chest relinquished weight.
Thank God I can finally breathe.

Passion flowed throughout my soul.
To a point I'll drown no more.
For today I can only see.
A world with dreams and goals.

Clutched my hand through thick and thin,
You found my spirit deep within.
For you, I bled, cried, and prayed.
Knowing one day I would thrive again.

Lord, use my scars for those to save.
Hardwood heaven, so much I gave.
But without you I wouldn't be,
The person who is resilient, strong, and brave.

For the love of God I gave my life,
For this I know deep down inside.
That even though we may fall,
By grace we carry on, and alas...
                    WARRIORS RIS3.

THE END...NO, THE BEGINNING.

The R.I.S.E. Playbook

Introduction

In Warriors RIS3, Peyton Murphy gave her longtime
teammate, Kelly Janssen, a version of The R.I.S.E.
Playbook—a guide written by their high school
basketball coach, Coach T, that reflected on lessons
they learned through their years on the court
together. The R.I.S.E. Playbook is a strategy to rise
after a fall and to continue to support those in our
care through their own hardships. Kelly used The
R.I.S.E. Playbook to not only navigate through her own
adversity but also to help Grace.

This playbook is a guide, workbook, journal, book
club prompts, devotional, or whatever you choose for
it to be for you. It includes suggested scripture
readings and reflection, a playbook application
of questions, and space for you to write down your
thoughts and prayers. The last section is a "Season
Recap," which dives deeper into the story of Warriors
RIS3. Journaling was key in my healing process. I
hope utilizing this section will help you express the
emotions and thoughts you may be experiencing in this
season instead of allowing them to consume you or to
cause you to turn to unhealthy ways to cope.

What started simply as a poem and personal therapy
for me, turned into a story I never imagined would
be told in a book. Don't be afraid to allow God to use
your story. You never know who may need to hear it. I
hope the story in Warriors RIS3 and the lessons, tips,
and applications in The R.I.S.E. Playbook help you take
action to build resiliency to RISE, rebound, and move
forward as you face adversity, uncertainty, and defeat.

Hardwood Heaven: Chalk Talk

Much like Coach Kelly Janssen, when I began prioritizing basketball and my own selfish ambitions over God's will, pride and ego took the lead in my life. The path I chose without including God ultimately led to a dead end, though I couldn't see it then. Instead of using basketball as a tool (the way God intended it to be), I turned it into my own personal idol. It wasn't until I found myself lost in the darkness, unable to navigate my way home, that I finally turned back toward the only true light.

If you have ever felt alone, discouraged, anxious, depressed, not enough, or felt like you had no hope to go on, you are not alone. The only reason I overcame the storms I faced was because Jesus pulled me out of those dark waters. It's difficult to keep fighting when you feel you are drowning and surrounded by darkness. Think about when Jesus was crucified. Hope felt lost on Good Friday, and the world was dark and silent on Saturday. But then came Sunday and Jesus' resurrection. Keep hope in the darkness because the light is coming.

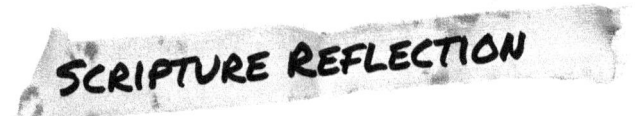

SCRIPTURE REFLECTION

Read John 1:1-18 and John 3:16-21

How do these two scriptures reveal who Jesus is and why He came into the world?

Define "The Word" according to the Bible.

Describe God's love for us according to John 3:16-21.

How do you define your identity?

Is there anything in your life you have made into an idol?

What are your gifts and strengths?

What unique skillset do you bring to your team?

What or who do you place your hope in?

The Defeat: Identifying Junk Defenses

Going undefeated in basketball is rare. It doesn't happen in life. At some point, you're going to face adversity. In basketball, junk defenses are designed to disrupt—causing confusion, frustration, and chaos. They target your weaknesses and force you out of rhythm. They're unpredictable, messy, and hard to prepare for. As Peyton explains to Kelly, life can throw junk defenses at you when you least expect them.

This may seem obvious, but it's important to first identify the junk defense you are facing. It's easy to misread what is actually defeating you, especially if you were not prepared. You might think you're dealing with a box-and-1, only to come down the court the next possession and realize it's actually a 1-3-1 zone. Life operates in a similar way. The junk defense may not be the root of why we were defeated.

Like the story of The Fall, Satan deceived Adam and Eve to question their identity in God. Satan still does this to us today. He uses confusion, misdirection, and fear to keep us off-balance—just like a junk defense. We must not only recognize the schemes we're up against but also stay grounded in who we are in Jesus. Just like in basketball, victory doesn't always come from avoiding adversity. It's about learning how to face it with faith, focus, and perseverance.

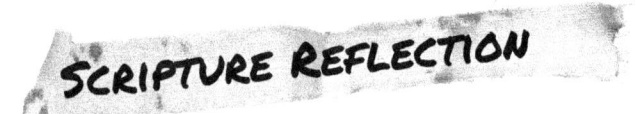

SCRIPTURE REFLECTION

Read Genesis 3, Genesis 50:20, and Psalm 34:17-18.

What lies did the serpent tell the woman?

Why did Adam and Eve hide from God? Where in your life are you tempted to hide from God?

How do these scriptures help you understand God's presence in times of adversity?

PLAYBOOK APPLICATION

What junk defenses have challenged you recently?

Identify one action item you can implement to Survive and Advance.

Think about a hardship you previously experienced in your life. How did you overcome the hardship, and what did you learn?

Looking back at this particular defeat right now, what
drives you to learn and become better?

What unexpected good has come from this defeat?

Write down actionable ways you can rest, refresh, and
refocus.

R.I.S.E.: Improving your Verticality

I often use athletic tape in a variety of ways. Not
only do I use it as the obvious injury prevention,
rehabilitation, and stability, but I often use it for
labeling items. But, athletic tape has a much deeper
significance to me. Athletic tape represents resilience,
grit, and healing. It is there for strength and support
and to help you through your healing process. It is
also a great reminder the pain is only temporary.
In other words, the adversity you are facing and
the pain you are experiencing is only for a season.
Wearing athletic tape is not always comfortable, just
like the process of working through adversity is
not comfortable. Learn to become comfortable being
uncomfortable.

It only seemed fitting to use athletic tape to label The
R.I.S.E. Playbook. The R.I.S.E. acronym is a strategy the
Lord gave me to get up and continue on. My athletic
background and lessons I learned from the Bible have
taught me that when you fall you don't just stay down.
You get up. You move on. Next play. You rise

Failure is never easy, but God can use it to shape
you into the person He created you to be. Just as in
sports, setbacks don't mean the game is over forever.
Instead, it's an opportunity to adjust, grow, and rise
higher than ever before. When you choose to rise with
a heart fixed on Jesus, He strengthens your spirit and
teaches you through the process. Remember, your story,
including the messy parts, may be the exact playbook
someone else needs to rise, too.

SCRIPTURE REFLECTION

R: REDISCOVER YOUR WHY
I: IGNITE YOUR PASSION
S: STRENGTHEN YOUR SUPPORT SYSTEM
E: EMPOWER OTHERS

Read Micah 7:8, Isaiah 40:31, and Isaiah 60:1-3.

All three scriptures address rising out of adversity.
What common theme do you notice in how God equips us
during hardship?

How can these scriptures help you in moments when you
feel defeated?

Where in your life are you in need of feeling God's
presence?

PLAYBOOK APPLICATION

What are your dreams and goals?
If you must pivot, write down ways you can continue to pursue your goals.

If you are a caregiver to others, what are examples of strategies you may use to rise out of your adversity while helping others through theirs?

Before diving into The R.I.S.E. Playbook strategy, identify ways you can condition your ability to rise.

What adjustments do you need to make to rebound successfully?

List 3-5 healthy habits you can implement into your daily routine:

Rediscover Your Why:
Winning the 3 Key Stats

Like Coach T, Peyton, and Kelly, I also share the same basketball philosophy of controlling the controllables and winning the three key stats you can control in a game— turnovers, free throws, and rebounds. During seasons of hardship or loss, it's easy to turn inward, cast blame, or let negativity take over. But that's when it's most important to lock in on the things you can control. In life, the three key "stats" to focus on are: mental focus and poise, executing the easy and mastering your routine, and your effort and attitude. Win those, and you give yourself the best shot at victory.

Rediscovering our why involves rediscovering our identity in Jesus. In denying ourselves, we surrender our own desires, ambitions, and identity shaped by the world, and instead find our true purpose and value in Jesus. We discover who we truly are: beloved, redeemed, chosen, forgiven, and made new in Him.

We don't know what junk defenses we will face in life, but if we win the three key stats and rediscover our why, we can face any challenge and overcome it. We aren't going to avoid adversity, but we can equip ourselves to rise through it. Getting up when you fall is the easy part of this process. But keeping your focus on Jesus during the height of the storm is the challenge.

Rediscover your why:

1. Lose with grace.
    - Come to Jesus with a humble heart.
    - Take accountability.
    - Don't play the blame game.
    - Forgive others, and forgive yourself.

2. Watch game film and review the stats.
    - Take a self inventory on where you might be missing the mark.
    - Rediscover your identity. Where are you in your relationships? With God?

3. Study your playbook & communicate with your coach.
    - Open those lines of communication.
    - Talk to your mentors.
    - Focus on your WHY.

Read James 1:2-18, Matthew 14:22-33, Luke 9:23-27.

What does Jesus reveal to you about trusting Him?

How do these verses encourage you about uncertainty?

What does Jesus teach us about faith in the midst of hardship and fear?

How do these passages remind you of your "why," and how might God be using your current struggles to realign your heart with His purpose for you?

List ways you can control the 3 key stats:

After reviewing your game film and stats, what do you need to be accountable for?
·What can you improve on?
·Was there anything you could have done or handled differently?

Write down the name of someone you need to forgive. Why do you need to forgive this person? (note: this may be yourself)

What is your WHY?

What would your mentor and/or hero say to you in this season?

What book are you reading or what podcast have you listened to this week? What did you learn?

Go for a walk and listen to uplifting music, an inspirational audiobook, or a leadership podcast 3-5 times this week. As you reflect, what insights did you gain?

Ignite Your Passion:
Focusing on the Fundamentals

Basketball is a game of technique and fundamentals.
One of the first lessons every player learns is the
importance of mastering the basics. No matter how
advanced you become, everything is rooted in the
fundamentals. When you hit a shooting slump, the
most effective way to find your rhythm again is by
returning to those core skills. It's in those moments
you also reconnect with your "why"—the purpose that
fuels your passion for the game. Stay locked in on
your why. Kelly understood this as a coach, but did she
understand this same principle in her personal life?

In basketball, mental conditioning is just as important
as physical training. These are some of the mental
conditioning methods I used as a player and coach;
visualization, staying positive in your thoughts and
words, calming your mind through breathing exercises,
and staying present in the moment. In the end, the
strongest players are those who train their minds as
relentlessly as their bodies. Just like muscle memory,
if you lock in on the fundamentals and remember why
you started in the first place, you will ignite your
passion and build resilience to get you through tough
moments. Over time, your mindset will become second
nature.

Igniting your passion is about focusing on your
why and staying rooted in your foundation. Focusing
on your fundamentals will help you build a strong
foundation. If you have a strong foundation, your
house can still be rebuilt regardless of the damage

and scars you may endure. Even in the midst of the storm, never lose sight of your joy in the game. Remind yourself of the memories and moments that brought you joy. Let gratitude and joy be the glue that keeps you together as you face the storms ahead.

Ignite your Passion:

1. Go back to the basics.
 •Focus on the fundamentals.
 •Find ways to relax and recharge.
 •Don't continue to live in a season of pain.

2. Do the little things that don't show up on the stat sheet.
 •Build healthy habits.
 •Control the controllables.
 •Acts of kindness are healing.
 •Practice gratitude.

3.Search for your joy in the game.
 •Do the things that give you joy.
 •Feed your mind with positivity.
 •Silence the haters.

SCRIPTURE REFLECTION

Read Matthew 18:1-14, 1 Corinthians 9:24-27, and Philippians 4:6.

Write 1-3 takeaways you took from these passages?

Reflect on the values found in these scriptures—humility, discipline, prayer, and gratitude. In what 2–3 specific ways can you begin applying these in your life to ignite your passion?

What might change in your life if you trusted like a child, trained like an athlete, and made prayer your first response?

PLAYBOOK APPLICATION

What is your passion, and why do you pursue it?

What basic skills or fundamentals do you need to go back to and master?

What is your training routine for mental conditioning? If you don't have one, what are some action items you can implement?

Write down 3 things you are grateful for and why.

Think back to when you were a child. What brought you joy?

If you could give your younger self advice or a helpful pep talk, what would you say?

Strengthen Your Support System:
Building a Strong Help Defense

Basketball is a team game and cannot be won by a single player. Success requires trust, support, and reliance on your teammates. In the same way, life isn't meant to be lived in isolation. God didn't design us to carry our burdens alone; He created us to serve, support, and uplift one another.

Kelly was a defensive minded coach and player. Like her, my passion in basketball was found in defense. It's where I thrived as a player. But even the best defenders can't succeed without unity. Great team defense demands that everyone be on the same page, moving as one. When one player gets beat, others have to step in. Trust and communication are essential. A strong help defense isn't just a strategy...it's a mindset.

The same principle applies to life. We need each other. God placed people in our lives to walk with us and us with them, especially in times of struggle. Strengthening your support system is just as important as any game plan because overcoming adversity takes a strong help defense.

Strengthen Your Support System:

1. This is a team sport.
   - You are not alone.
   - We need each other to win.
   - Surround yourself with people who uplift you and are good for your soul.

2. Communicate on the court.
   - Keep an open line of communication with your teammates.
   - Share your feelings and what you are experiencing with a teammate.

3. Become a great teammate.
   - Make your relationships with your teammates a priority.
   - Team bonding is important.
   - Be present.
   - Listen to understand.
   - Put yourself in your teammate's shoes.

SCRIPTURE REFLECTION

Read Galatians 6:1-10, and Matthew 11:28-30, Philippians 1:3.

What does it look like to "carry someone else's burden"?

What burdens are you carrying that Jesus is inviting you to lay down at His feet?

How is God inviting you to both serve others and receive His rest in your own soul?

PLAYBOOK APPLICATION

Who is someone on your "team" who needs support? How can you support and encourage them?

How can you help your teammates win in life?

Identify ways you can develop new relationships or grow your current relationships.

Who is your mentor? What lessons have they taught you?

Empower Others:
Creating an Assist Mentality

The most beautiful basketball I've ever witnessed is
when a team flows effortlessly on offense—moving the
ball from one side of the court to the other without
wasting a single dribble and creating a wide-open shot
at the rim. When players operate in perfect precision
and unison, the result is not only efficient but
successful. Kelly and Peyton's team thrived by playing
this particular style of winning basketball.

A vital stat to winning basketball is the assist. A
high team assist count is more than just a stat; it's
a testament to teamwork, selflessness, and empowering
others. Much like basketball, we don't succeed alone in
this life. We need assists from our teammates.

Peyton exemplified what it means to empower others
through the way she supported Kelly. Her love for
Kelly was deep and unwavering, yet she wasn't afraid
to offer tough love when it was needed most. She
equipped Kelly with the strength, support, and tools to
move forward. Even through her own struggles, Kelly
passed this same gift of empowerment on to Grace.
Though she doubted her own impact, Kelly became a
guiding force, helping Grace discover her own path.
Each of us carries the same calling to empower others
even in the middle of our own storms.

Empower Others:

1. Know and buy into your role.
   - You are unique.
   - You have unique gifts that contribute to the team's success.

2. Pay it forward.
   - Serve others.
   - Think outside of yourself.

3. Help your teammates become the best they can be.
   - Plant the seeds. You may never see the harvest, but plant the seeds anyway.
   - Encouragement breeds confidence.
   - Don't be afraid of your own voice.
   - Your vulnerability will help others RISE by creating trust and connection.

SCRIPTURE REFLECTION

Read Romans 12, Isaiah 58:10, and 2 Corinthians 1:4.

Who is God calling you to be a light in their
darkness?

What gifts are you using to serve others?

How has God shown up with His comforting presence
during your season of pain?

If you could carry out a random act of kindness for someone, what would it be? Take action.

Identify a way you can serve your community.

Think of a time when you were at one of your lowest lows. What advice and encouragement would you give to yourself now?

Who are the individuals in your life you can mentor?

The Comeback: Finding Joy in the Process

Reminiscent of both Kelly and Peyton, I tore my ACL several years ago. I can confidently say it was one of the worst injuries I have ever experienced. Overcoming adversity and making a comeback are like the healing and recovery process of an ACL injury. It's grueling, it tests you, and it takes a lot of perseverance.

Epic comebacks in a basketball game are a process and take a lot of mental toughness. Unfortunately, you can't erase a 20-point deficit with one, single shot. Comebacks are built possession by possession. Every offensive play, every defensive stop matters. Success comes from valuing each moment on the court and staying locked in. The same is true in life. Just like in basketball, comebacks aren't instant. They are a process. You have to stay grounded, take it one step at a time, and focus on winning the present.

The beauty of an epic comeback isn't just in the result, it's in who you become in the journey. Similar to recovering from an ACL injury, the process forces you to grow and to strengthen your resilience, patience, discipline, and perspective. Every setback is a chance to take you to a depth of yourself you didn't know you had. Whether on the court or in life, the process of coming back shapes you. And often, what you gain through the struggle is far more valuable than what you lost.

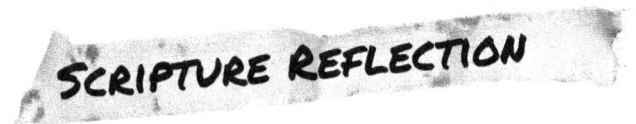

SCRIPTURE REFLECTION

Read Romans 5:3-5, Philippians 4:13, Jeremiah 29:11 and Psalm 20:4-5.

Are the desires of your hearts, your goals, and your plans aligned with God's will?

How can you learn to rejoice in your sufferings?

How do these three passages challenge you to deepen your understanding of perseverance and hope?

Which of these verses do you identify the most with right now? Why?

PLAYBOOK APPLICATION

What R.I.S.E. tips can you apply in your own life when facing setbacks?

Describe an epic comeback you have witnessed. Why does this particular comeback story inspire you?

What joy have you discovered from this process?

What did you learn about yourself through this journey?

What are you hopeful for?

Season Recap

I'll never forget one of the last seasons I coached
college basketball. It was one of the final games
of the season. We were on the road in a hostile
environment. As our team was warming up, my assistant
coach picked up a game program. We flipped through it
and noticed a section written as a season recap.

I remember thinking, Why a recap? The season's not
over yet. But there it was—written as if the game
had already been played, they'd beaten us, and secured
their spot in the playoffs. There were still games left
in the season. A single loss could knock them out of
playoff contention. According to that recap, we were
counted out before the whistle had even blown. They
were going to put the nails in our coffin and bury us.

We were furious. The write-up became instant bulletin
board material. Although we were in the middle of a
losing streak and didn't qualify for playoffs, we still
had something left to prove. We had an opportunity
to upset them and spoil their plans. We were now
determined to do so.

I've never seen our team more fired up. We came out
strong, jumped to an early lead, and shocked both the
home team and their fans. But then a controversial
call rattled us. We lost our composure and our
confidence. Doubt crept in. We lost our edge... and
ultimately, the game.

I think about that moment regularly. How often in
life do we find ourselves stuck in a losing streak and

begin to believe it's over? When life doesn't unfold the way we imagined, it's easy to question whether things can ever change. We lose sight of the hope we once had. Our confidence gets shaken by someone or something. And just when it feels like we're making progress, an unexpected setback throws us out of rhythm again.

Kelly felt this way. Grace did, too. Both believed at some point in their story their life was finished. They couldn't envision a path forward. Just as they felt they were rebounding, something unexpected threw them off their game plan. Doubt took hold. They couldn't see their way back to the light.

But the truth is, there's always hope. Even when it feels like the final chapter's already been written. God has a plan in all of it—even the losing streaks. He will provide a way home. You may not see it, but you have to let Him light your way.

A season recap is not the end. Losing is not the end. It's a chance to grow by learning from your previous experiences. It's an opportunity to build a playbook for yourself and others. It's a reminder your past does not define you, and God is not finished with you. He's preparing you for the next play. Take your thoughts captive. Stop listening to yourself and start declaring God's Word over your mind. Allow God to turn your pain into purpose.

SCRIPTURE REFLECTION

Read Luke 15:11-32 and Ephesians 2:1-10.

How do you define grace?

How does the Bible define God's grace?

In the Parable of the Prodigal Son, why was the older son upset with his father when his brother returned home? How can you compare this to us today?

How have you seen God's grace at work in your life?

When God answers your prayers, do you respond with celebration of His name or pursuit of your own?

PLAYBOOK APPLICATION

Which character in Warriors RIS3 do you most identify with and why?

Symbolism is a key element in Warriors RIS3 — was there a specific symbolic section that stood out to you? Why?

Which struggle did Kelly wrestle with the most, and how did she overcome it?

What basketball analogy can you apply to your own life?

What characteristics did you appreciate the most about Peyton, and why?

What was the difference in how Kelly handled her adversity in comparison to how Grace handled hers?

Who is your Peyton? Are you a Peyton for someone else?

Grace faced many adversities in her life. What was her motivation to overcome all of the junk defenses thrown at her?

What did you learn most from Warriors RIS3?

If you reviewed your seasons of life, what is the greatest lesson you have learned?

About the Author

Terri S. Van Slyke is a former NAIA collegiate basketball player, former USCAA college basketball coach, and former sports journalist. Her passion for mentoring and leading college students stems from her 20-year career working in higher education in admissions and student recruitment, student affairs, academic advising, marketing, and athletics, as well as her experience advising various student leadership groups and involvement with college ministries. Terri credits her athletic experiences and her faith in Jesus as the inspiration for her book, Warriors RIS3. She believes basketball teaches powerful lessons and provides athletes a skillset that can be applied to many facets of life. Terri strives to impact, inspire, and empower others to learn to RISE amid adversity by a strategy that she created called The RISE Playbook. She has presented this strategy to a variety of organizations, professional staff, and high school and college students.

An avid fan of sports, sneakers, and music, Terri was born in Kansas and raised in Albany, Missouri. She takes great pride in her Midwestern, rural roots. Terri earned her Bachelor of Arts degree in Communications from Kansas Wesleyan University and her Master of Arts degree in Coaching and Athletic Administration from Concordia University Irvine. She currently resides in Central Kansas with her beloved cat, Marvin.

In Loving Memory of Mama Sweet Pea
March 23, 1946 - September 25, 2025

"But behind all your stories is always your mother's story, because hers is where yours begins."
- Mitch Albom

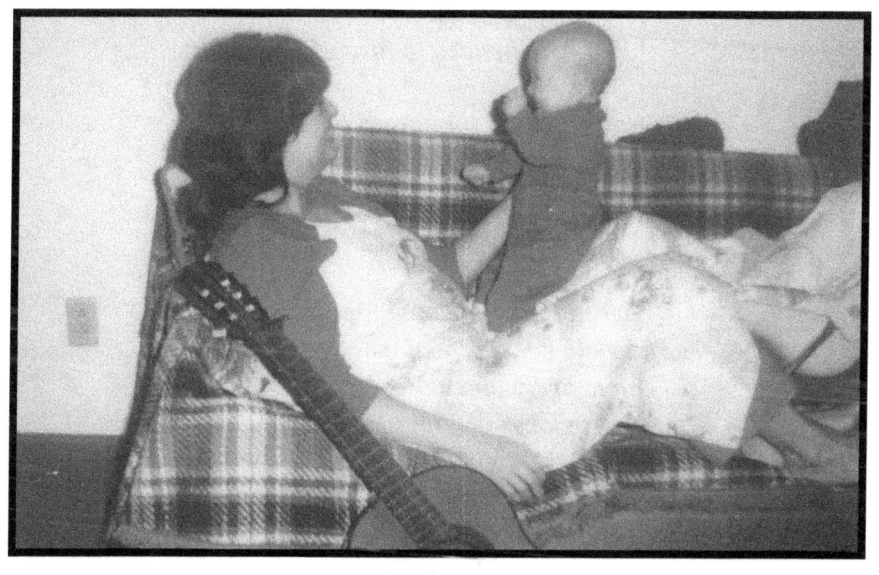

Trust in the Lord with all your heart and lean not on your own understanding; in all your ways submit to him, and he will make your paths straight.

Proverbs 3:5-6 NIV

RISE Up

By Terri S. Van Slyke and Sheryl A. (Lykins) Van Slyke

"No matter what our circumstances are,
God is worthy of our praise."
You wrote this and I read it,
On one of my darkest ever days.

You went home to be with Jesus,
After years of pain and suffering.
I'm sad and yet I'm thankful,
You're in heaven to forever sing.

From your song lyrics and my thoughts,
This poem together we now write.
But I would be amiss if I did not admit,
I wrote this while I cried.

I'm searching for my inner strength,
But my heart is heavy with despair.
I can hear you tell me to "lean on Jesus.
He loves you and He cares."

"The Lord is my light and my courage.
He's with me all day long.
He's my strength when I'm discouraged.
He's my salvation, He's my song."

"We must rise up and declare it,"
Were the lyrics that you wrote.
In a song to spread the gospel,
To give people peace and hope.

I'll do my best to take on your mission.
I won't stop until my day is done.
Because in the end, we'll meet again,
In the presence of the Son.

I'll do what you said, Mama,
I'll encourage everyone to RISE,
To search their heart to find Jesus,
So all may have eternal life.